Blueprint
ONE

Students' Book

Brian Abbs
Ingrid Freebairn

Longman

Contents

Preview

UNITS 1-5

📟 Listen and follow the conversation.

In Units 1–5 you will learn how to:

- introduce yourself and others
- greet people and say goodbye
- talk about nationality
- identify objects
- give personal information

You will also learn:

the days of the week, the alphabet, colours and numbers 1–100.

1 Names

Hi! My name's Laura.

Hello! I'm Adam.

Her name's Laura.

His name's Adam.

1 Ask the names of ten students in your class and write them down.

A: What's your name?
B: My name's . . . / I'm . . .

2 Answer these questions.

Which names begin with the letters C or S?
Which names end with the letters A, E or O?
Which name (or names) is most common?
What's your partner's name? (Her name's . . . / His name's . . .)

3 Talk to three other students and complete the chart with the names.

A: What's your mother's name?
B: (Her name's) Maria.

	Mother	Father	Brother/Sister
Student 1 Student 2 Student 3			

4 Tell the class about people's names.

Student 1 is Antonio. His mother's name is . . .

5 In pairs, ask and answer.

A: What's the name of your school/college/company?
bank? favourite café?
favourite pizza place?

B: It's called . . .

Note
It's called . . . **not** ~~Its name is~~ . . .

GRAMMAR FOCUS:

Subject pronouns	Possessive adjectives
I	my
you	your
he	his
she	her
it	its

Verb *to be* **Genitive *s***
I'm = I am my mother**'s** name
You're = You are my parents**'** name
She's = She is **Genitive *of***
the name **of** my school

What does the *'s* stand for: *is* or genitive *'s*?
1. What's 2 My father's name 3 My name's
4 My textbook's called

6 In pairs, ask and say who the people are.

A: Who's that?
B: It's Mr Gorbachev./I don't know.

Mike Tyson	Mrs Cory Aquino	Crocodile Dundee
Mr Gorbachev	Mrs Thatcher	(Paul Hogan)
Mother Teresa	Steffi Graf	Tom Cruise

7 READING

Read and answer.

1 What's Jorge's name in English?
2 What's Christine called for short?
3 Is Chris a boy's name or a girl's name?

My name's Jorge.

His name's Jorge. He's called George in English.

My name's Chris.

Her name's Christine but she's called Chris for short. Chris is a boy's name and a girl's name in English.

8 WRITING

Write down three boys' names and three girls' names in your language and write what they are in English.

Margareta is Margaret in English.

2 Greetings and goodbyes

5

1 📼 Listen to the conversations and match them with the pictures.

2 Introduce people informally.

YOU: Claudia, this is Tony.
CLAUDIA: Hello, Tony.
TONY: Hello./Hi.

3 Use the clocks to greet each other with *Good morning, Good afternoon* **or** *Good evening.*

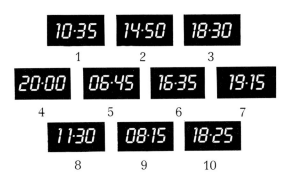

4 Use the calendar to write the days of the week in the correct order.

Sunday   Thursday   Wednesday   Tuesday
Saturday   Friday   Monday

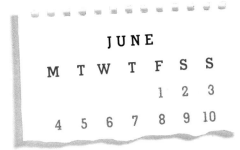

📼 Now listen and repeat the days.

Note
The days of the week always begin with a capital letter. Is it the same in your language?

5 Answer the questions.

What day is it today?
What day is it tomorrow?
What day was it yesterday?
What days are 'the weekend'?
On what days are your English classes?

6 Say goodbye on different days of the week.

A: Bye! See you on . . . day.
B: Yes, O.K. Bye.

7 📼 SPEECHWORK

Listen and underline the stressed syllables or words.

How do you <u>do</u>   Hello   How are you
Good morning   Good afternoon
Morning   Good evening   Good night
Goodbye   See you on Monday

COMMUNICATION FOCUS:
Greetings and goodbyes

Formal	*Informal*
How do you do?	Hello./Hi!
Good morning.	Morning!
Good afternoon.	Afternoon!
Good evening.	Evening!
Goodnight.	Night!
Goodbye.	Bye!

What are some formal and informal greetings in your language?

---

8 📼 LISTENING

Listen and complete the conversation.

CHRIS: Hello, Adam. . . . you?
ADAM: . . . fine, . . .   And . . .?
CHRIS: I'm O.K. Adam, . . . Karen, a friend from Leeds.
ADAM: . . . , Karen.
KAREN: Hi!
ADAM: Sorry, Chris but I must go.
CHRIS: That's O.K.
ADAM: See you . . .
CHRIS: O.K. . . .
ADAM: Thanks. And the . . . .!

9 Practise the conversation in groups of three. Use your own names.

10 Say goodbye to other students.

A: Bye! Have a nice day/evening/weekend.
B: Thanks. And the same to you. See you tomorrow/on . . . day.

3
Nationalities

1 Find the letters for these countries on the map.

Italy Argentina France Greece Spain
Britain The USA Brazil Turkey China
Japan The USSR Portugal West Germany

2 What are the capital cities of the countries?

3 Ask and say where you are from.

A: Where are you from?
B: I'm from (France). Are you from (France) too?
A: Yes, I am./ No, I'm not.

4 ▣ SPEECHWORK

Which stress pattern can you hear? Is it 1, 2 or 3?

1 <u>Bri</u>tain 2 Ja<u>pan</u> 3 <u>I</u>taly

China Portugal Turkey Brazil Germany

5 Guess the nationality of the people in the photographs. Choose from the list.

Japanese Italian American Spanish
French Turkish Chinese Brazilian
German British Greek

A: I think the girl/woman/boy/man in picture . . . is . . .
B: No, I think she/he's . . .
A: And I think the couple/people in picture . . . are . . .
B: No, I think they're . . .

6 In pairs, check the answers on page 141.

A: Is she/he British?
B: Yes, she/he is./No, she/he isn't. She/He's . . .
A: Are they Chinese?
B: Yes, they are./No, they aren't. They're . . .

7 Talk about yourselves.

I'm (Italian) and I'm from (Turin).

8 ▣ LISTENING

What language do you think it is?

A: I think it's Spanish.
B: Yes, it is./No, it isn't. It's Portuguese.

1	Spanish	Portuguese	Greek
2	Japanese	Chinese	Thai
3	Dutch	Swedish	German

7

GRAMMAR FOCUS: Verb *to be* – present simple

Positive	*Negative*	*Question*
I'm French.	I'm not English.	Am I English?
She/He's English.	She/He isn't French.	Is she/he English?
It's Portuguese.	It isn't Spanish.	Is it Spanish?
We're Italian.	We aren't English.	Are we English?
They're Chinese.	They aren't French.	Are they English?

Write the full form of the words.
1 it's 2 isn't 3 we're 4 they're 5 aren't

Make these statements into questions.
1 She's American. 2 They're English. 3 You're French.

9 Quiz: Where is it?

A: Where's the Eiffel Tower?
B: It's in Paris./It's in France.

1 the Eiffel Tower?
2 the Prado Museum?
3 the Great Wall?

4 the Empire State Building?
5 the Taj Mahal?
6 the Kremlin?

10 In which countries do they speak these languages?
Spanish   Portuguese
German   French   English

Write sentences about three world languages.
People speak Spanish in . . . ,
. . . and . . . .

11 READING AND WRITING

Read about Youcef and then write about yourself.

'My name's Youcef. I'm Algerian and I'm from Algiers. Languages are my hobby. I speak Arabic, French, English, Hungarian and Russian – and I also speak a little German! My English is quite good but my Russian is very bad.'

My name's . . . I'm . . . and
. . . from . . . I speak . . . and . . .

8

4 Objects

1 In pairs, match these words with the objects in the picture. Which objects are not in the picture?

a desk	a pen	a book
a diary	a telephone	a notebook
an envelope	a stamp	a chair
an orange	an apple	a mug
a lamp	a bag	a key
a wallet	an umbrella	a letter
a drawer	a pencil	an address book

2 Discuss the objects in pairs.

A: What's that?
B: It's a wallet.

A: What are those?
B: They're pencils.

9

3 🔊 SPEECHWORK

Listen and underline the stressed syllables.

<u>pen</u>cil <u>en</u>velope wallet apple diary orange
telephone address

GRAMMAR FOCUS

Indefinite article		Definite article	Plurals
a desk	**an** apple	**the** pen	(the) pen**s**
a pen	**an** orange	**the** apple	(the) apple**s**

When do you use *an*?
What letter makes a word plural?

Prepositions of place

The pen is **in** the bag. The pen is **on** the desk.

---

4 In pairs, check where things are in the picture.

A: Where's the apple/the wallet?
B: It's in the drawer/bag.
A: Where are the letters?
B: They're on the desk.

5 🔊 Listen and say the letters of the alphabet.

Aa	Bb	Cc	Dd	Ee	Ff
Gg	Hh	Ii	Jj	Kk	Ll	Mm
Nn	Oo	Pp	Qq	Rr	Ss	Tt
Uu	Vv	Ww	Xx	Yy	Zz

6 Complete the list of vowels.

A E . . .   .

7 Choose an object and ask a student to spell it.

A: Carla, how do you spell 'wallet'?
B: W.A.L.L.E.T.

8 Find two things in your pocket or handbag. Ask another student what they are called in English and how to spell them.

A: What's this in English?
B: It's a purse.
A: How do you spell it?
B: P.U.R.S.E.

A: What are these in English?
B: They're keys.
A: How do you spell 'keys'?
B: K.E.Y.S.

9 🔊 LISTENING

Listen and say what present Adam got for his birthday from his mother and father. Choose from the following.

a cassette recorder
a CD (compact disc) player
a radio.

10 Ask and say what colour the objects in the picture on page 9 are.

red	orange	yellow
pink	blue	purple
green	brown	beige
grey	white	black

A: What colour is the telephone?
B: It's . . . .

11 Memory game

Look at the picture for one minute. Close your book. Write down the things you can remember. You have two minutes to write your list. Now compare it with your partner's.

5

Personal information

Mr A.J.Birch,
Flat 2,
16, George St,
York,
YO1 5ES

The Palms HEALTH CLUB

SURNAME: *Birch*
FIRST NAMES: *Adam Jermaine*
ADDRESS: *Flat 2, 16, George St, York, YO1 5ES*
TELEPHONE NUMBER: *0904 776351*
AGE: *19* SIGNATURE: *A.J. Birch*

1 ▣ Listen and say the numbers.

1 one	11 eleven	21 twenty-one
2 two	12 twelve	22 twenty-two
3 three	13 thirteen	30 thirty
4 four	14 fourteen	40 forty
5 five	15 fifteen	50 fifty
6 six	16 sixteen	60 sixty
7 seven	17 seventeen	70 seventy
8 eight	18 eighteen	80 eighty
9 nine	19 nineteen	90 ninety
10 ten	20 twenty	100 a hundred

2 ▣ Write the numbers you hear.

3 Ask your partner her/his full name and how she/he spells it.

A: What's your surname?
B: It's (Birch).
A: How do you spell it?
B: (B.I.R.C.H.)
A: What are your first names?
B: (Adam Jermaine).

4 Find out your partner's address.

What's your address?
How do you spell it?/the name of the road?

5 Find out your partner's telephone number.

A: What's your telephone number?
B: It's . . .

Note
O is pronounced *oh* /əʊ/
77 = *double seven*

6 In pairs, ask questions to complete your list of telephone numbers. Do not look at your partner's list. Ask questions like:

What's Alan Baker's telephone number?
What's the telephone number of Blake's Restaurant?

STUDENT A

NAME *Alan Baker*
TELEPHONE
NAME *Claudia Bellini*
TELEPHONE *010 39 2 29404347*
NAME *Adam Birch*
TELEPHONE *0904 776351*
NAME *Blakes Restaurant*
TELEPHONE
NAME *British Airways*
TELEPHONE *01 8974000*
NAME *British Rail*
TELEPHONE

STUDENT B

NAME *Alan Baker*
TELEPHONE *643731*
NAME *Claudia Bellini*
TELEPHONE
NAME *Adam Birch*
TELEPHONE
NAME *Blake's Restaurant*
TELEPHONE *835791*
NAME *British Airways*
TELEPHONE
NAME *British Rail*
TELEPHONE *0904 642155*
NAME
TELEPHONE

7 Ask and say how old you are.

A: How old are you?
B: I'm nineteen.

Note
You can say: *I'm nineteen.* or *I'm nineteen years old.* The second is used more often in written English.

8 In pairs, ask how old these people are.

A: How old is she/he?
B: I think she/he's about . . .

9 Find out and write down the full names, addresses, telephone numbers and ages of three other students in the class.

10 🔲 LISTENING

Listen and complete the form for Adam's friend Chris.

APPLICATION FORM
(please use BLOCK CAPITALS)

Surname ....

First names ....

Title (*please tick*)   Mr ☐   Mrs ☐   Miss ☐   Ms ☐

State if (*please tick*)   Married ☐   Single ☐   Divorced ☐

Address ....

.... Postcode ....

Telephone number .... Age ....

11 READING AND WRITING

Read about Adam and write about yourself in the same way.

'My full name is Adam Jermaine Birch. Jermaine is my grandfather's name. I'm nineteen years old. I'm British. My address is Flat 2, 16, George Street, York. I'm not married.'

Now use the information from Exercise 9 to write about another student.

ABOUT NAMES AND ADDRESSES

How to talk about people by name

Mr Birch	Miss/Ms Martinelli
Adam Birch	Laura Martinelli
Adam	Laura
(but **not** Mr Adam)	(but **not** Miss Laura)

Mrs/Ms Jackson
Betty Jackson
Betty
(but **not** Mrs Betty)

How to write addresses on envelopes

Mr A.J. Birch,	Laura Martinelli,
Flat 2,	c/o Gibson,
16, George Street,	1, Hull Road,
York, YO1 5ES	York, YO4 2HT

Notes
16, George Street **not** George Street, 16.

The postcode is important because it gives exact details of the area, street and house where you live. It comes after the name of the town or city, e.g. *York, YO1 5ES.*

What do you think these are short for?
1 Rd   2 St   3 c/o

Rewrite the information below to address an envelope.
EX3 5LT   P.J. Fisher   105   Mr   Exeter Hill St

What a Surprise!

Think of a friend and give them a surprise! YOU phone and tell us about your friend: name, address, age, telephone number and so on. WE ask you a simple question about the nationality of a famous person. IF you give the right answer, your friend wins a wonderful prize!

Phone us now on 885 885.

Fill in this form and have your information ready!

WHAT A SURPRISE! COMPETITION FORM

Friend's name: ....

Friend's home town: ....

Friend's telephone number: ....

Friend's age: ....

Choice of present for friend: (please tick)

☐ a Radio York Diary ☐ a Radio York T-shirt

☐ a Radio York sports bag

Your name: ....

Your address: ....

Your telephone number: ....

1 READING

Read the advertisement for 'What a Surprise!' and note the correct answer.

1 Who telephones Radio York?   a) you b) your friend
2 Who answers the
  'nationality question'?   a) you b) your friend
3 Who gets the prize?   a) you b) your friend

2 ▣ LISTENING

Listen to a telephone call to 'What a Surprise!' and answer the questions.

1 What's the caller's name?
2 Is her friend a boyfriend or a girlfriend?
3 What present does she want for her friend?
4 What is the 'nationality question'?
5 What is the answer?

3 Complete the competition form with information about one of your friends and think of a 'nationality question'.

Example
What nationality is John McEnroe?
What nationality is Cory Aquino?

4 ROLEPLAY

In pairs, roleplay a telephone call to Radio York. Student A telephones to try to win a prize for a friend. Student B is the Disc Jockey and asks a 'nationality question'.

DISC JOCKEY	CALLER
Say hello. Ask the name of the caller and where he/she is from.	
	Say who you are and where you are from.
Ask what the friend's name is.	
	Say what your friend is called.
Ask where he/she is from.	
	Say where your friend is from.
Ask how old he/she is.	
	Say your friend's age.
Ask what present the caller wants for his/her friend.	
	Say what present you want.
Ask the 'nationality question'.	
	Answer the question.
If right, say 'You win a . . . for your friend'.	
	Say thank you and goodbye.

5 WRITING

Read the text below and write a similar paragraph about your friend for the Radio York Magazine.

THIS WEEK'S winner of Radio York's popular phone-in programme 'What a Surprise' is Jonathan Hunt. Jonathan is twenty-one. He's from York. His present from his girlfriend Maggie in Leeds is a T-shirt. Congratulations Maggie and Jonathan!

19

Check

UNITS 1-5

1 Choose the correct answer.

Example
1 A: What . . . your name?
   a) 's b) are c) am
   [a circled]

1 A: What . . . your name?
   a) 's b) are c) am

2 A: Are you English?
   B: Yes, I . . .
   a) is b) am c) are

3 A: Is your name Adam?
   B: Yes, . . . is.
   a) she b) he c) it

4 A: Is he from London?
   B: No, he . . .
   a) isn't b) not c) is

5 A: What nationality is she?
   B: She's . . .
   a) Germany b) German c) Dutchland

6 John, . . . is Anneli, a Danish friend.
   a) here b) it c) this

7 Karen is a friend . . . Leeds.
   a) in b) from c) of

8 A: What's this in English?
   B: It's . . . address book.
   a) a b) the c) an

9 A: Where . . . the envelopes?
   a) are b) is c) do

10 The stamps are . . . the drawer.
   a) on b) to c) in

2 Write the questions.

Example
1 What's your name?
   My name's Helen.

1 . . .?
   My name's Helen.
2 . . .?
   Her name's Jenny.
3 . . .?
   His name's Mark.
4 . . .?
   Her name's Mary.
5 . . .?
   The name of the college is York College
   of Education.

3 Choose the odd word out.

Example
1 blue red chair yellow
   [chair circled]

1 blue red chair yellow
2 envelope stamp letter umbrella
3 book mug notepad address book
4 afternoon evening hello morning
5 Greek France Italy Germany

4 Rewrite the sentences using *he, she, we* or *they*.

Example
1 Laura is from the USA.
1 She's from the USA.

 1 Laura is from the USA.
 2 Adam is from Britain.
 3 Paolo and Bruno are from Italy.
 4 Lydia and I are from Brazil.
 5 Yvette is from France.
 6 Hans and Steffi are from Germany.
 7 Placido is from Spain.
 8 Bernard and I are from Switzerland.
 9 Maria is from Portugal.
10 Mr Osoko is from Japan.

5 Write the nationality adjectives.

Example
1 USA   *American*

 1 USA   . . .
 2 Brazil   . . .
 3 Japan   . . .
 4 Spain   . . .
 5 Portugal   . . .
 6 China   . . .
 7 Argentina   . . .
 8 Mexico   . . .
 9 Italy   . . .
10 France   . . .

6 Rearrange the sentences in the right-hand column to make a conversation.

Example
1 *Good morning.*   *c)* *Good morning.*

1 Good morning.	a) 3, Park Road, Cambridge.
2 What's your surname?	b) No, I'm not.
3 And your first name?	c) Good morning.
4 Are you married?	d) Johnson.
5 What's your address?	e) David.

7 Write the apostrophes in the correct place.

Example
1 Im Karen.
1 *I'm Karen.*

1 Im Karen.	4 Whats your mothers
2 Shes a friend from work.	name?
3 Theyre from Brazil.	5 Hes Adams friend.

8 Choose the correct answer to complete the conversation at a railway station.

Example
ADAM: Hello, Chris.
CHRIS: a) Good morning. (b) Hello.

ADAM: Hello, Chris.
CHRIS: a) Good morning.   b) Hello.

ADAM: How are you?
CHRIS: a) Fine, thanks.   b) Thank you, well.

ADAM: Chris, this is my mother.
CHRIS: a) How do you do, Mrs Birch.   b) Hi! Mrs Birch.

ADAM: a) Chris is a friend from work.
        b) It's a friend from work.

MRS BIRCH: Oh, yes. Nice to meet you.

ADAM: Ah, here's our train. Bye, Chris!
CHRIS: a) Goodnight!   b) Goodbye!

9 Write capital letters where necessary.

Example
1 my name's adam.
1 *My name's Adam.*

1 my name's adam.
2 i'm from paris.
3 he's italian.
4 good morning, mrs gibson.
5 my name's john. what's your name?

10 What are these days of the week?

Example
1 naymod
1 *Monday*

1 naymod
2 ustadey
3 auysartd
4 urstadhy
5 eysneawdd

CHECK YOUR PROGRESS

Add up your score. How well did you do?

Easy exercises?
  (e.g. *2, 3* . . .)
Difficult exercises?
  (e.g. *1* . . .)
Problems? (e.g.
  verb tenses . . .
  spelling . . .
  prepositions . . .)

LEARNING TO LEARN 1: Asking for help

When you start to learn a new language, these phrases are useful:

- What does (*blueprint*) mean?
- What is (*tavola*) in English?
- How do you say (*Achtung!*) in English?
- How do you spell that?
- How do you pronounce that?
- Can you say that again, please?

1 Find a new word in Unit 6. Ask your teacher what it means.
2 Think of a useful word in your language. Ask your teacher what it is in English and how to spell it.
3 Think of a useful expression in your language. Ask your teacher how to say it in English.

Preview

UNITS 6-10

🎧 **Listen and follow the conversation.**

Do you work near here?

No, I'm a student at the university.

Do you like York?

Yes, very much. It's a lovely city.

Where do you live in the States?

I come from the west coast, from San Diego in California.

Yes, but not very well.

Really? I've got a cousin in California. He's a surfer. Can you surf?

Look, I must go. Give me a ring some time.

O.K. Bye!

Answer *Yes, No* or *Don't Know*.

1 Adam and Laura are in a café.
2 Laura works in York.
3 Laura is from the USA.
4 Adam can surf.

In Units 6-10 you will learn how to talk about:

– skills and abilities
– the family
– jobs and lifestyles
– likes and dislikes
– geographical location
– cities of the world

6
Skills and abilities

1 Choose the correct sentence for each picture.

Yes, I can, a little.   I can't see.
I can't hear you very well.   I can't read her writing.

GRAMMAR FOCUS: Modal verb *can* (ability)

Positive	*Negative*
I can speak English.	I can't (cannot) speak French.

Question	*Short answer*
Can you speak English?	Yes, I can.
Can you speak French?	No, I can't.

Note
Can doesn't change with *he, she, they*, etc.
e.g. *Can I / you / she / he / we / they speak English?*

Levels of ability

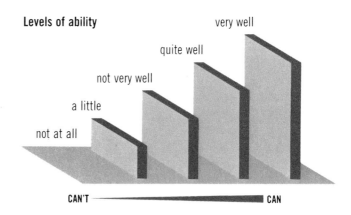

CAN'T ———————————————→ CAN

2 In pairs, use the information above to talk about your language abilities.

French   Italian   Spanish   German   Russian   English

A: Can you speak French?
B: No, not at all./Yes, a little./Yes, but not very well.
   What about you?
A: Yes, quite well./Yes, very well.

3 ⌨ SPEECHWORK

Listen and say if you hear /kæn/ or /kən/.

Yes, she can.   I can speak English.   He can speak French.
Yes, I can.   Can you speak Italian?   What can you do?

What can you do?

SPORTS

- swim
- ski
- windsurf
- ride a horse
- play tennis
- play volleyball

PRACTICAL

- cook
- drive
- change a wheel
- repair a puncture
- type
- use a computer
- change a plug

ARTISTIC

- act
- dance
- play the guitar
- play the piano
- draw
- sing

4 Use the chart to talk about your skills in pairs or groups. Add to each column if necessary.

A: Can you swim?
B: Yes, I can. What about you?
A: Yes, but not very well. Can you ski?
B: No, I can't.

5 Tell the rest of the class about the things that your group can do well.

Gisela can play the guitar quite well and she can sing too.

6 WRITING

Write about your skills. Join your sentences with *and, but* and *or*.

SPORTS: I can swim and windsurf very well.
PRACTICAL: I can type quite well but I can't use a computer.
ARTISTIC: I can't sing or dance but I can play the piano a little.
LANGUAGES: I can speak German quite well but I can't speak French very well and I can't speak Spanish at all.

Note
The phrases *very well, quite well, a little* and *at all* come after the object in a sentence, e.g. *I can't speak French **very well***.

7 READING AND 📼 LISTENING

Read the results of a survey about the ability of British people to speak French.

How well can the Brits speak French?

The British are not a nation of linguists, as the results of this survey show.

	AGE		
	15-34	35-54	55+
Can read a menu	38%	31%	22%
Can ask directions	40%	28%	21%
Can read a French newspaper	9%	10%	7%
Can have a simple conversation	32%	22%	15%
Can understand a TV or radio programme	8%	7%	6%
Can speak French fluently	3%	3%	2%
Can do none of these	50%	63%	78%

How do you score in English?

Now listen to a British person living in Paris. Look at the survey above and note down what the person can and can't do.

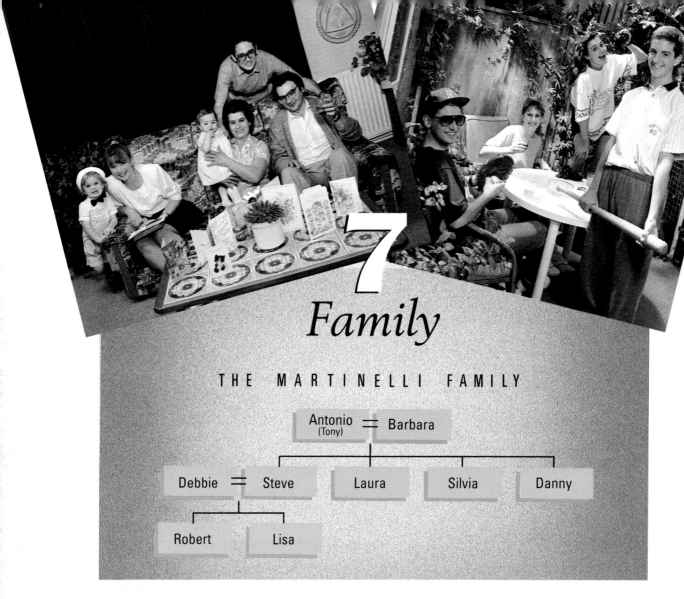

7
Family

THE MARTINELLI FAMILY

```
                  Antonio ══ Barbara
                  (Tony)
        ┌───────────┬──────────┬──────────┐
   Debbie ══ Steve  Laura   Silvia     Danny
    ┌────────┴────────┐
 Robert            Lisa
```

1 In pairs, use the family tree and the words below to identify all the people in the photographs.

mother/father/parents
sister/brother
daughter/son/child/children
wife/husband

A: I think they're Laura's mother and father.
B: And that's her brother, Steve.

2 Use the Grammar Focus box to ask and answer about Laura's family.

A: How many brothers has she got?
B: She's got two.
A: Has she got any sisters?
B: Yes, she has.
   She's got one.

GRAMMAR FOCUS: Verb *have got*

Question	Short answer	Positive and negative
Have you got any brothers or sisters?	Yes, I have. No, I haven't.	I've got two brothers. I haven't got any sisters.
Have they got any children?	Yes, they have. No, they haven't.	They've got four children. They haven't got any children.
Has she/he got any children?	Yes, she/he has. No, she/he hasn't.	She/He's got two children. She/He hasn't got any children.

What are the full form of the words?
1 they've   2 haven't   3 she's got   4 we've   5 hasn't

21

3 Complete the sentences about Laura's family.

Tony and Barbara are Laura's . . . and . . .
They've got two . . . and two . . .

Steve is Debbie's . . .
Debbie is Steve's . . .
They've got two . . . , a boy called Robert and
a baby girl called Lisa.

Laura's got two . . . and one . . .
Her . . . are called Tony and Barbara.

4 ▣ SPEECHWORK

Listen and repeat. Notice the sound /ð/.

this   they   their   mother   father   brother

5 Use the words below to describe relationships in Laura's family.

grandmother/grandfather aunt/uncle
niece/nephew   cousin

1 Laura to Lisa   4 Lisa to Danny
2 Danny to Lisa   5 Barbara to Robert
3 Robert to Laura   6 Tony to Lisa

1 Laura is Lisa's aunt.

6 Write down the first names of four or five people in your family. Exchange lists with another student. Ask and answer about the people on the lists.

A: Who's Emma?
B: She's my cousin.

7 ▣ LISTENING

Listen to Adam talking to Laura about his family. Use the names below to draw his family tree.

William   Michael   Dorothy   Mary   Jim

8 Talk in pairs about your own family.

A: Have you got any brothers or sisters?
B: . . .
A: What are their names?
B: . . .
A: How old are they?
B: . . .
A: What about your parents?
  How old are they?
B: . . .
A: And are your grandparents alive?
B: . . . .

9 READING

Read about Cher, a famous American film star, and answer the questions.

1 What nationality were her ancestors?
2 What was her first husband's name?
3 What was the name of their first hit record?
4 How many children has she got?

Cher's real name is Cherilyn La Pierre. Her family ancestors were French, Turkish, Armenian and Cherokee Indian. Her first husband was called Sonny Bono and together, as 'Sonny and Cher', their record, *I Got You, Babe*, was a big hit in 1965. Cher won an Oscar for Best Actress in the film *Moonstruck* in 1988. She has got two children, a daughter called Chastity by her first husband and a son by her second husband called Elijah Blue.

ACTRESS   SINGER   OSCAR WINNER – BORN 1946

GRAMMAR FOCUS:

Verb *to be* – past simple

Present
My grandmother is Irish.
My grandparents are Irish.

Past
My grandmother was Irish.
My grandparents were Irish.

10 WRITING

Write a paragraph about your family. Say if you come from a big family or not. Mention any interesting ancestors you have got. Start like this:

I come from a big/small family. I've got . . .

8

Jobs and lifestyles

1 READING

Listen and read about people from different parts of the world. Then answer the questions.

Who has got
grown-up children? a baby daughter? two teenage children?

Who lives
at home? alone? with friends? with her mother?

Who lives
in a flat? in the country? in a hostel?

Who is
a student? a musician? a bus driver? a journalist?

Who works
at an airport? in a factory? for the government? on a farm?

Shirley Norris is a telephone operator from Houston, Texas.
'I'm divorced and I live with my mother. She's quite old and can't look after herself. My children are all grown-up.'

Brenda Churchill comes from England.
'I'm a bus driver and a housewife. I live with my two teenage children near Leeds. My husband works in a factory.'

Carlos and Helen Garcia are Spanish.
'We live in the centre of Madrid in a flat. I'm a journalist and my wife is a musician. She plays the violin for the Spanish National Orchestra.'

Michel Moulin comes from France.
'I live at home with my family. We live in the country near Perpignan. I work on a farm.'

Selma da Silva comes from Recife, Brazil.
'I'm Brazilian. I work for the airline VARIG. I work at the check-in desk at the airport in Recife. I live with my husband and baby daughter in a small flat in Recife.'

GRAMMAR FOCUS: Present simple –

I / You / We

Question	Positive
What do you do?	I'm a bus driver.
Where do you work?	I work in a factory.
Where do you live?	We live near Leeds.
	Negative
	We don't live in London.
	Short answer
Do you live in the centre (of . . .)?	Yes, I/we do.
	No, I/we don't.

What word comes before *you* in all these questions?

2 🔊 SPEECHWORK

Listen and underline the stressed syllable or word.

Where do you <u>work</u>?   Where do you live?
What do you do?   Where do you come from?

Kevin Johnson comes from Ireland.
'I live with friends in a hostel in Belfast. We're all students at the university.'

Vera Laucas is Portuguese.
'I live in a flat in a suburb of Lisbon. I live alone and I work for the government.'

3 ROLEPLAY

Two of the people in the photographs meet on holiday. Act out their conversation.

QUESTIONS
What/name?   Where/come from?
What/do?   live with/family?

RESPONSES
Oh, really?   That's interesting.

GRAMMAR FOCUS: Present simple –

He / She / They

Question	Positive
What **does** she/he do?	She's a bus driver.
Where **does** she/he work?	She/He work**s** in a factory.
Where do they live?	They live in Belfast.
	Negative
	He **does**n't live in Leeds.
	They don't live in London.
	Short answer
Does she/he work in a factory?	Yes, she/he **does**.
	No, she/he doesn't.
Do they live in a flat?	Yes, they do.
	No, they don't.

What letter occurs in all forms of the third person singular?

4 Choose one of the people in the photographs. Other students ask *Yes/No* questions to find out who it is.

A: Does he/she live alone?
B: Yes, he/she does.

5 🔊 LISTENING

Listen and say which of the people in the photographs is talking. How do you know?

6 Ask your partner about a friend from another city or country and take notes.

A: My friend's called . . .
B: Oh, yes. Where does she come from?
A: She comes . . .

7 WRITING

Write a paragraph about your partner's friend or a member of your family.

9
Likes and dislikes

Do you like it?

No, not much. It's too modern.

Really? I love it.

COMMUNICATION FOCUS: Expressing likes and dislikes

Do you like it?
Yes, I do. I love it.
Yes, I like it very much.
It's O.K.
No, not much./No, I don't like it very much.
No, I don't. I hate it.

1 Complete the chart with names of people and things you like.

	I like . . .	My partner
PERSONALITIES Male personality: Female personality: Politician: Rock band:	Prince	No
ENTERTAINMENT TV series: Types of film: (horror, war, romantic, science fiction, comedy, etc)		
HOME AND LEISURE Household jobs: (washing up, cooking, cleaning, shopping, etc) Leisure interests: (going to parties, playing cards, eating in restaurants, reading, watching TV, keeping fit, etc)		

GRAMMAR FOCUS:

Subject pronouns	Object pronouns
I	me
you	you
he	him
she	her
it	it
we	us
they	them

I (don't) like it/cooking.
I (don't) like him/Prince.

Note
The verbs *like, hate, love* and *enjoy* are often followed by *-ing*, e.g. *I like shopping. I hate cooking.*

2 Ask if your partner likes the people and things in your chart. Write *Yes, No,* or *O.K.* in the answer column.

A: Do you like Prince?
B: No, I don't. I hate him./ He's O.K.

5 READING AND WRITING

Read the advertisements and choose one you like.

● I am a 23-year-old biology student. I am interested in photography, travelling and music. I am looking for a penfriend who can speak English, from any country in the world.
Cezary Toma, 40- 2002 Katowice, ul Sikorsuiego 16 m 20, Poland

● I am an English teacher in a secondary school near Lisbon in Portugal. My pupils aged 14-18 are looking for penfriends so that they can practise their English.
Maria de Luz, Escola Secundaria No. 2, Estrada Da Estacao, 2615 Alvrerca, Portugal

● I am interested in writing to people all over the world, especially in Scandanavia, Japan, Spain or Italy. I am 22 years old and I like literature, cycling, reading and studying nature.
Christine De Laperriere, 2/242 Place R. Coeur de Lion, 86000 Poitiers, France

Write a short letter in reply. Say who you are and where you come from. Mention your job (or studies), your age and your interests.

Put your address here on the right.

> Flat 25,
> 4, Chester Road,
> Hanwell,
> London,
> W7 2TA,
> England

3 Tell the class about some of the people and things you and your partner disagree about.

I like Prince but Anna doesn't like him.

4 READING AND 🔲 LISTENING

Read the 'Dateline' advertisement. Then listen to three interviews. Note each man's name, age, job and interests. Then say which you think is the best partner for the woman in the advertisement and explain why.

● **TALL, SLIM, English girl,** 20ish.
Likes romantic films and French food.
Interested in classical music.
Also keen on energetic walks and travelling. Am I the person for you?
Box N438

Date your letter here under the address.

Start your letter here on the left.

> 17th May

Dear Cezary,

My name is Yoshiko Kawamura and I come from Osaka, Japan. I am twenty years old. At the moment I am a student of English in London. I like going to the cinema and listening to music. Do you like Whitney Houston? I like her very much and I have got all her albums. I am also interested in photography and travelling. Of course, I like studying English very much.

Please write to me here at my address in London and tell me about your life in Poland. I hope that we can be penfriends.

Yours sincerely,

Yoshiko Kawamura

Yoshiko Kawamura

Write your name clearly below your signature at the end of your letter.

Cities of the world
What are they like?

This week Ann Collins visits York and San Diego.

York is a beautiful old city in the north-east of England on the River Ouse. It is not far from Leeds. It is a very interesting place to live. It has many historical buildings and museums but it is most famous for its cathedral, called York Minster.

NORTH SEA

River Ouse
York ●
Leeds ●

ENGLAND

London ●

USA

CALIFORNIA

Los Angeles ●

PACIFIC OCEAN

San Diego ●

San Diego is a city in Southern California on the west coast of the USA, on the Pacific Ocean. It is not far from Los Angeles. It has a big harbour, beautiful beaches and a famous zoo. Many people think it is the best place to live in California.

10
Places

1 READING

Read the texts and complete the information.

Name of city:	York	San Diego
Name of country/state:		
Position:		
Attractions:		

2 In pairs, write a list of places in your country.

Give the name of:
a tourist city
a big town in the north
an old university
a beautiful building
a boring town
a town near the sea
an industrial city
a small town in the south
a modern (new) university
an ugly building
an interesting town

In groups, compare your lists. Are they the same?

Note

The definite article *the* is used before oceans, seas and rivers, e.g. *the Pacific Ocean, the North Sea, the River Ouse.*

GRAMMAR FOCUS:
Prepositions of place

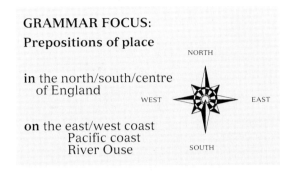

in the north/south/centre
of England

on the east/west coast
Pacific coast
River Ouse

3 In pairs, ask and say where the following places are.

Bilbao	Madrid	Izmir
Naples	New York	Acapulco
Paris	Malaga	Thessaloniki

A: Where's Bilbao?
B: It's in the north of Spain.

4 What do you think the following cities are famous for?

Florence Sydney Paris Madrid
Rio de Janeiro Chartres

Use the following to help you.

beaches	nightlife	shops	food
harbour	football team		cathedral
museums and art galleries			

Florence is famous for its museums and art galleries.

5 LISTENING

Listen to someone describing a city in Exercise 3. Which city is the speaker describing?

6 Write down all the adjectives you can find in this unit. Put them in opposite pairs where possible, e.g. *big/small.*

7 SPEECHWORK

Listen and underline the stressed syllable.

beautiful interesting industrial gallery
historical restaurant cathedral university

8 ROLEPLAY

STUDENT A
You meet Student B on a train in your country. Use these questions to have a conversation.

Where do you come from?
Where is that exactly?
What's it like?
Do you like living there?

STUDENT B
You come from York and are travelling in Student A's country. Answer Student A's questions. Then return the questions.

Note
What's it like? = What sort of place is it?
To be like is used to ask for descriptions of people, places and things, e.g. What is he/she/it like?

9 WRITING

Write a paragraph about a city or town you know well. Say where it is, what it is like and if it is famous for anything.

10 Did you know?

A British newspaper recently asked its readers to vote on places they liked. Here are the results.

BEST PLACE IN BRITAIN FOR A WEEKEND BREAK	BEST EUROPEAN COUNTRY TO VISIT	BEST COUNTRY TO VISIT OUTSIDE EUROPE
1 York	1 France	1 The United States
2 Lake District	2 Italy	2 Canada
3 London	3 Greece	3 Australia
4 Bath	4 Austria	4 India
5 Edinburgh	5 Spain	5 Thailand

Make a similar list for your country.

Fluency

UNITS 6–10

1 READING

In pairs, A and B, read your text. (Do not read each other's text.) Write the answers to these questions.

1 What is Victor's full name?
2 How old is he?
3 Where does he live?
4 How many brothers and sisters has he got?
5 What does his father do?
6 What does his mother do?
7 What does he do?
8 Does he like his job?
9 How does he spend his money?
10 Does he like school?
11 Does he speak English well?

COLOMBIA

Quito
ECUADOR

BRAZIL

PERU

Lima

BOLIVIA

PACIFIC OCEAN

CHILE

STUDENT A's TEXT

Victor Raul Manani is ten years old. He lives in a 'pueblo joven' (a shanty town) near Lima on the west coast of Peru. He's got three brothers and two sisters. His father is dead. His mother sells potatoes in the market. Victor sells chewing gum and hats to people in cars. 'I work because I need to eat,' says Victor. 'I don't like selling things in the streets but I like making money. I make quite a lot. I spend it on shoes, school books and clothes but I give some money to my mother. I like school and learning English. I can speak a little English now.'

STUDENT B's TEXT

Victor Jorge Manani is twelve years old. He lives in a 'pueblo joven' (a shanty town) near Quito in Ecuador. He's got two brothers and one sister. His father washes up in a café. His mother sells fish in the market. Victor sells cigarettes and hats to people in cars. 'I work because I need to eat,' says Victor. 'I like selling things in the street because I like making money. I make quite a lot. I spend it on sweets, comics and going to the cinema. I spend all my money. I don't like school but I like learning English. I can speak it quite well.'

2 Find out if you have the same information. Look at the instructions for Student A and Student B.

STUDENT A

Use your notes about Text A to tell Student B about Victor. Student B will interrupt you if his/her information is different.

A: His full name is Victor Raul Manani.
B: No, it isn't. His full name is Victor Jorge Manani.

STUDENT B

Listen to Student A and give different information where necessary.

A: His full name is Victor Raul Manani.
B: No, it isn't. His full name is Victor Jorge Manani.

One of the texts is true. Which one is it? Why do you think so? The answer is on page 141.

Plaza San Martin, Lima

3 🔲 LISTENING

Listen to two people talking about the city of Lima and make notes under the following headings.

Name of city:
Description:
Location:
Main attractions:

4 WRITING

Use your notes from Exercise 3 to write a short paragraph about Lima.

Lima is the capital of Peru. It is a tourist city and an . . .

Check

UNITS 6-10

1 Choose the correct answer.

Example
1 A: . . . you ski?
   B: Yes, a little.
   (a) Can   b) Have   c) Are

1 A: . . . you ski?
   B: Yes, a little.
   a) Can   b) Have   c) Are

2 He . . . in the centre of Madrid.
   a) live   b) does live   c) lives

3 . . . she live in Milan?
   a) Is   b) Does   c) Do

4 A: I like this music.
   B: Really. I . . . like it.
   a) don't   b) not   c) no

5 She . . . with her parents.
   a) don't live   b) doesn't live   c) live not

6 . . . like living in America?
   a) You do   b) Do you   c) Does you

7 A: Has she got any brothers?
   B: Yes, she . . . I think she's got two.
   a) has   b) have   c) has got

8 My brother hates . . .
   a) to shop   b) shopping   c) shop

9 A: Do you like Anna?
   B: Yes, I like . . . very much.
   a) her   b) she   c) him

10 He can speak . . .
   a) very well English
   b) English very good
   c) English very well

2 Rearrange the words to make sensible sentences.

Example
1 you cycling like do?
1 *Do you like cycling?*

1 you cycling like do?
2 much like very she him doesn't.
3 live they do where?
4 his he parents with does live?
5 this I like music don't.

3 Complete the sentences with a, *an* or the.

Example
1 I've got . . . uncle and two aunts.
1 *I've got an uncle and two aunts.*

1 I've got . . . uncle and two aunts.
2 She lives in . . . centre of Vienna.
3 London is . . . big city.
4 . . . cathedral in York is very old.
5 Paris is in . . . north of France.

4 Complete the text with the correct preposition.

at   in (x2)   on   from (x2)   with
of (x2)   for

'My parents come (1) *from* Scarborough, a town (2) . . . the east coast (3) . . . England but I live and work (4) . . . Leeds. I'm a secretary and I work (5) . . . an international company. My office is quite near the centre (6) . . . the city. I live (7) . . . a flat (8) . . . three friends. My boyfriend, Tom, is a student (9) . . . the Polytechnic. The Polytechnic is not far (10) . . . my flat.'

5 Match the opposites.

mother   south
morning   sister
love   modern
near   small
interesting   father
big   hate
brother   boring
old   uncle
aunt   far
north   evening

6 Rearrange the sentences in the right-hand column to make a conversation.

Example
1 What nationality are you?   *g) I'm Spanish.*

1 What nationality are you?
2 Where do you live in Spain?
3 Where exactly is that?
4 What do you do?
5 Where do you work?
6 Are you married?
7 What does your husband do?
8 Have you got any children?
9 How old are they?
10 Do they learn English at school?

a) In a big hospital in Barcelona.
b) I'm a nurse.
c) I live in a place called Badalona.
d) Yes, we've got two boys.
e) It's a town outside Barcelona.
f) One's seven and the other is nine.
g) I'm Spanish.
h) Yes, I am.
i) Yes, they do.
j) He works in a shoe factory.

7 Answer the questions using the correct pronoun.

Example
1 Do you like your job?
1 Yes, I like it very much.

1 Do you like your job?
2 Do you like your grandparents?
3 Do you like your aunt?
4 Do you like your nephew?
5 Do you like your cousins?
6 Do you like your new flat?
7 Do you like your uncle?
8 Do you like your niece?
9 Do you like your school?
10 Do you like me?

8 Rewrite the paragraph putting in the correct punctuation (full stops and capital letters).

'My name's Laura . . .

'my name's laura and i'm twenty-two years old i come from california in america but i'm in york at the moment i'm a student at the university york is a very beautiful old city and i like living here very much'

CHECK YOUR PROGRESS

Add up your score. How well did you do?

Easy exercises?   . . .
Difficult exercises? . . .
Problems?   . . .

LEARNING TO LEARN 2: Talking about grammar

Here are some important 'grammar' words:

Grammar word	Example	Names of verb tenses	
noun	chair, girl	*present simple*	I live
article	a, the	*present continuous*	I am living
verb	be, have, write	*past simple*	I lived
adjective	good, bad	*going to future*	I am going to live
adverb	well, badly	*simple future*	I will live
preposition	on, in	*present perfect*	I have lived

What are these words?
1 boy   2 go   3 beautiful
4 an   5 slowly   6 open
7 brown   8 for   9 speak

What are these tenses?
1 he is working   2 they like
3 I have worked   4 she wanted
5 I am going to have

Preview

UNITS 11-15

🔊 Listen and read the captions.

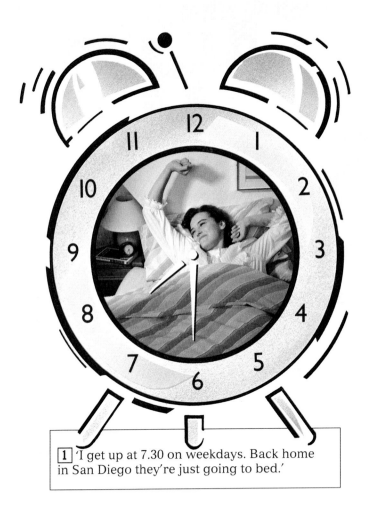

1 'I get up at 7.30 on weekdays. Back home in San Diego they're just going to bed.'

2 'I cycle to college. It only takes me ten minutes.'

Answer *True* or *False*.

1 Laura gets up at seven.
2 She walks to college.
3 She usually works in the library.
4 The library opens at eight o'clock.
5 Laura is living in a hostel.
6 Laura likes her room.

In Units 11–15 you will learn how to:

– tell the time
– say what time things happen
– describe your daily routine
– talk about journeys
– describe your home
– talk about present activities

J.B. MORRELL

Library

Library Opening Times

Monday – Friday:
from 9.00 to 22.00

Saturday:
from 9.00 to 17.15

3 'I usually go to the library in the morning. It opens at 9.'

4 'I'm staying with a couple called Mr and Mrs Gibson. Their daughter's working in Zambia. I've got her room.'

5 'It's a nice room. There's a big table near the window. I like working there.'

34

Coppelia

Northern BALLET Theatre
Artistic Director CHRISTOPHER GABLE

York THEATRE ROYAL

TUESDAY 9 – SATURDAY 13 MAY
PERFORMANCE STARTS 7.30 p.m.
TICKETS FROM £4.50

First Choice
ODEON YORK 23040

Week from Friday 10 March

ODEON 1 : GORILLAS IN THE MIST (15)

Fri, Mon–Thur 2.10, 5.00, 8.05

Sat 4.20, 7.15, 10.00

Scarborough and York → Londo

Principal train services 15 May to 1 October

Mondays to Fridays				Saturdays		
Scarborough depart	York depart	Kings Cross arrive		Scarborough depart	York depart	Kings
0600	0822					
0627e	0650	0854		0627	0635	08
	0725	0933			0735	09
	0750e				075	10
	0800	095				5

Celebrate!
Sue's birthday party
On 23rd June At 9 o'clock
At 28, Fulford Rd, York

7.35 BEADLE'S ABOUT. Jeremy Beadle with pranks and practical jokes.
8.05 MURDER SHE WROTE. With Angela Lansbury, as matronly sleuth Jessica Fletcher, plus Efrem Zimbalist Jr, Richard Roundtree and Dale Robertson.
9.00 SARACEN*. Action-man series.
10.00 ITN NEWS Sport 10.15 LWT Weather.

11
Times

1 📼 **Listen and repeat the times.**

It's one o'clock.   It's quarter past one.   It's twenty to two.

It's ten past one.   It's half past one.   It's quarter to two.

2 In pairs, ask and say the times.

A: What time is it?
B: It's seven o'clock.

 1
 2
3
 4
5
6

Note

- You can also use numbers to say the time, e.g. *9.15 = nine fifteen*.
- In Britain, the twenty-four-hour clock, e.g. *23.30*, is only used for programmes, timetables and notices.
- *10 a.m. = ten o'clock in the morning*
- *3 p.m. = three o'clock in the afternoon*
- *6 p.m. = six o'clock in the evening*
- *11 p.m. = eleven o'clock at night*
- *Noon, midday = 12.00 hours*
- *Midnight = 24.00 hours*

3 VOCABULARY

Number the words below from the shortest time to the longest time. Use a dictionary.

day   hour   fortnight   year   second
month   minute   week   century

1   second

Ask and answer questions about each of the time words.

A: How many seconds in a minute?
B: Sixty.
A: How many . . . in a . . .?

4 READING

Look at the programmes, timetable advertisements and invitation on the left. In pairs, ask and answer these questions.

What time is:
– the ballet?
– the film?
– the train to London?
– the party?
– the news?

A: What time is the ballet?
B: It's at half past seven (in the evening).

GRAMMAR FOCUS:
Prepositions of time

at eleven o'clock   **on** Sunday
at night/midnight   **in** the morning
from 8 a.m. **to** 11 a.m.

Which preposition?
1 . . . noon   2 . . . the afternoon
3 from 10 a.m. . . . 5 p.m.   4 . . . 1.30 p.m.
5 . . . Tuesday

---

5 ▣ LISTENING

You are going to York tomorrow. You want to be there by 10 o'clock. You phone King's Cross station to find out the train times.

Listen to the information and choose a suitable train. Tell your partner what time your train leaves King's Cross and what time it arrives in York.

6 Ask and answer about the times on the college noticeboard. Use the verbs below.

open   close   start   finish   leave   arrive

A: What time does the library open?
B: It opens at nine a.m./nine o'clock in the morning.

7 Answer questions about your school, college, office or factory.

What time:
– does it open in the morning?
– do you arrive?
– do you leave?
– does it close in the evening?
– do your English classes start?
– do they finish?

8 READING

Read the information below and answer the questions.

1 What time do banks open and close in Britain?
2 Do they open on Sunday?
3 What time do shops close?

ABOUT OPENING AND CLOSING TIMES IN BRITAIN

Post offices open at 09.00 and close at 17.30 from Monday to Friday. They close on Saturday at 12.30.

Banks open at 09.30 and close at 15.30 from Monday to Friday. A few banks open on Saturday morning. In big cities, *Bureau de change* offices open every day until quite late in the evening.

Shops usually open at 09.00 or 10.00 and close at 17.30 or 18.00. They do not usually close for lunch except in small towns. Most shops are closed on Sunday and national holidays.

---

9 WRITING

Now write similar information for visitors to your country.

J.B. MORRELL
Library

Library Opening Times
Monday – Friday:
from 9.00 to 22.00
Saturday:
from 9.00 to 17.15

Film Club

WEDNESDAY 2 p.m.
MAIN THEATRE
James Dean
in the classic film
East of Eden

APPROX 90 MINUTES
Entrance £1.50

UFC

UNIVERSITY FOOTBALL CLUB

FOOTBALL MATCH
Derwent College
v.
Halifax Polytechnic
Saturday 3.00p.m.
at Kendon Park
Bus leaves college
at 1.30p.m.
Arrives back
at 7.00p.m.

12

Routines

1 Imagine you are Laura. Match the correct sentence with each picture.

1 I have a shower and get dressed.
2 I usually go to the library in the morning.
3 I have lunch in the cafeteria.
4 I go home at five o'clock.
5 I always get up at seven thirty.
6 I go to bed at eleven thirty but I'm never asleep before midnight.
7 After supper I go out with friends.
8 I have breakfast at eight thirty.

GRAMMAR FOCUS: Zero article

No article (*the/a/an*) is used:
- with certain places after *go to*:
  I go to school/work/college/bed/church every day.
- with meals:
  I have breakfast/dinner/supper at nine.
  Lunch is at one.
- with *home*:
  I go home at five.

2 In pairs, ask and answer about Laura.

A: What time does Laura get up?
B: She gets up at seven thirty.
A: What does she do after that?
B: She has a shower and gets dressed.

Use these cues:
What time/have breakfast?
What/do in the morning?
Where/have lunch?
What time/go home?
What/do after supper?
What time/go to bed?

3 Write down eight questions to ask about your partner's daily routine. Then ask the questions and note the answers.

1 What time do you get up?
2 What . . .

4 Look at your partner's answers. Do you do the same things at the same time or not? Tell the class.

Carlos gets up at six thirty but I get up at seven.
We both have lunch at twelve thirty.

H

G

GRAMMAR FOCUS: Adverbs of frequency

always   usually   never   often   sometimes

Write the adverbs in order of frequency from *never* to *always*.
never   ....   always.

Position of adverbs in a sentence
She **always** gets up at seven thirty.
She **usually** goes to the library in the morning.
She's **never** asleep before midnight.

Does the adverb of frequency normally come before or after the main verb? Is this always true?

5 ▦ LISTENING

Listen to Adam talking about his daily routine. How often does he do things?

ACTIVITY	always	usually	often	sometimes	never
Get up at 7.30: Have a big breakfast: Leave home at 8.15: Get home before 7: Go out in the evenings: Go to bed before midnight:					

6 Write six sentences about Adam's day.

1 He usually gets up at seven thirty.

7 READING

Read about a nurse on night duty. Use the verbs below to complete the text about his daily routine. You can use some verbs more than once.

watch   finish   start   have
go   read   get up

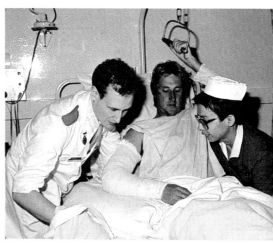

I'm a nurse at St Mary's Hospital. At the moment I'm on night duty. I . . . work at 9.30 p.m. and . . . at 8 a.m. Then I . . . home and . . . breakfast. I usually . . . the newspaper and . . . television a little and then I . . . to bed. I . . . at about 4 p.m. I sometimes . . . shopping, then I . . . supper. After that I . . . to the hospital. That's a typical day – or night – for me!

Which verb is used most frequently?

8 WRITING

Write a paragraph about your typical day. Start new sentences with *Then I . . .*, *After that I . . .*, *After lunch/work/school I . . .*

I always get up at seven and have a shower. *Then* I have breakfast and go to work. *After that/After work* I sometimes go shopping.

13
Journeys

Before you read

Where is the man?
What time of day is it?

A
LONG
DAY'S
JOURNEY
INTO
WORK

Do you think *you* have a long and boring journey to work? Well, David Ross takes over seven hours every day to get to and from work. That's 1,610 hours a year!

David Ross, a 32-year-old accountant, lives with his wife and two children in Leeming, a small country village near York in the north of England. But his job is in the centre of London, 400 miles (640 km) away in the south.

Every day David leaves home at five o'clock in the morning, drives three miles to his local railway station and catches the 5.30 train to York. At York he takes the 6.12 InterCity Express to King's Cross in London. From there he goes by underground to Liverpool Street Station and then walks to his office.

The whole journey takes three hours and fifty minutes. He gets home at nine o'clock in the evening. What a life!

Why does he do it? David smiles: 'Because I like my job in London b[...] I like living in the north and I like travelling by train!'

1 READING

Complete the information about David.

> Name:
> Age:
> Job:
> Home town:
> Place of work:
> Distance to and from work:
> Method of transport:
> Journey time:

GRAMMAR FOCUS:
Preposition *by* and means of transport

I usually go to work	**by** bicycle/train/car/ bus/underground.
I never travel	**by** plane/train/boat.
I always	walk to school/work/ college. drive. cycle.

2 Ask and answer the questions about David's journey.

A: How does he get from his home to the local station?
B: He goes by car./He drives.

1 from his home to the local station?
2 from York to King's Cross in London?
3 from King's Cross to Liverpool Street Station?
4 from Liverpool Street to his office?

3 🔲 LISTENING

Listen and note how long the following people take to travel to college or work.

1 John Gardener
   an engineer from Leeds
2 Sara Anderson
   a London solicitor
3 Joan Walker
   a doctor from Newbury

Talk about the answers in pairs.

A: How long does it take John to get to work?
B: It takes him . . .

4 ROLEPLAY

STUDENT A
You are Mrs Ross. Use the article about your husband to answer the radio reporter's questions.

STUDENT B
You are a reporter for Radio York. Use these cues to interview Mrs Ross.

What time/your husband get up?
How/travel to London?
How long/the journey take?
What time/get home in the evening?
Why/not/move to London?

5 Complete the survey for three students.

Journey to school/ college/work	Student 1	Student 2	Student 3
Method:			
Distance:			
Time:			

A: How do you usually get to school/college/ work?
B: I go by . . ./I walk.
A: How far is it?
B: It's about . . . kilometres, etc.

Compare the results of your surveys to find out how most people in your class get to work or college.

6 WRITING

John Ellis is a cycle messenger in London. He lives in north London and works in the centre, near Liverpool Street Station. Imagine his day. Write a paragraph about his journey to work and his daily routine. Use the words below to help you.

collect   deliver   letter   packet

The home

1 Name the rooms in the pictures. Choose from the following.

the sitting room
the dining room
the kitchen   the bathroom
the hall   a bedroom

2 Look at the pictures and find the following.

a door   a window   a floor
a ceiling   a wall   the roof

3 In pairs, say what there is in each room. Choose from the words below.

A: In the kitchen there's a table . . .
B: . . . and there are three chairs.

a table	a lamp
a sofa	a bookcase
a sink	a fridge
a wardrobe	curtains
a bath	a cooker
a bed	a shower
an armchair	a carpet
a TV	a cupboard
a chair	a washbasin
a toilet	a mirror
a dressing table	

4 🔲 SPEECHWORK

All these words have the letter *a* in them. How are they pronounced? Listen and see if you are correct.

lamp   hall   bath   wall
table   carpet

GRAMMAR FOCUS: There is/There are

Positive and negative	*Question*	*Short answer*
There's a chair.	Is there a chair?	Yes, there is.
There isn't a TV.	Is there a TV?	No, there isn't.
There are two tables.	Are there any tables?	Yes, there are.
There aren't any cupboards.	Are there any cupboards?	No, there aren't.

In which type of sentences is *any* used?

5 Ask and answer about each other's homes.

How many rooms are there?
How many bedrooms are there?
Is there a dining room?
What's your bedroom like?
What colour is it?
What furniture is there in it?

4

5

6 WRITING

Read about the Gibsons' house, then draw a plan of your own home and write a paragraph describing it.

> 2
>
> The Gibsons have got a typical English house. There are three bedrooms and a bathroom upstairs, and downstairs there's a sitting room, a dining room and a kitchen. There's a garden at the back and the front, and there's also a garage. My room is quite small. It's yellow and white and there's a table near the window. There's also a large mirror near ~~which has a~~

7 ◻ LISTENING

Before you listen

Describe the house in the photograph. Where do you think it is? What sort of people live in it? Use the words below to help you.

mansion   swimming pool   patio   rich

Listen to someone describing the house in the photograph. What is unusual about it?

ABOUT LIVING STANDARDS IN BRITAIN

Today over sixty-three per cent of the population of Britain own their homes. Four out of five families live in houses rather than flats. A survey in 1987 showed the following results.

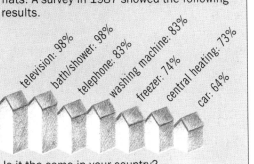

television: 98%   bath/shower: 98%   telephone: 83%   washing machine: 83%   freezer: 74%   central heating: 73%   car: 64%

Is it the same in your country?

For a closer look at the house in Exercise 7, turn to page 141.

42

1 have/a shower

2 play/the piano

3 listen/to music

4 watch/TV

5 make/coffee

15
Present activities

1 In pairs, talk about what the people are doing. Use the Focus box below to help you.

A: What's the girl/man in picture . . . doing?
B: She/He's . . .

GRAMMAR FOCUS: Present continuous

What	am	I	doing?	You're	writing a letter.
	are	you		I'm	
	is	he		He's	
	is	she		She's	
	are	we		We're	
		they		They're	

Spelling rules

start-starting   write-writing   run-running   lie-lying
learn-learning   make-making   get-getting   die-dying

What happens to verbs which end in *e*?
What happens to verbs which end in *ie*?
What happens to one-syllable verbs ending in one consonant, like *run* and *get*?

---

2 ▭ LISTENING

Listen and say what the people are doing.

3 Use a verb and an object to write sentences using *he* or *she* in the present continuous tense.

VERBS
write   read   listen to   clean   have   go

OBJECTS
the radio   a letter   a book   the news   to bed   lunch
the windows

1 She's writing a letter.

4 ▭ SPEECHWORK

Listen and repeat the phrases. Try to say /tə/ not /tuː/ each time.

going to work   going to school   going to bed
listening to music   listening to the radio

5 Mime an activity. Other students ask *Yes/No* questions to find out what you are doing.

A: What am I doing?
B: Are you cleaning something?
A: No, I'm not.
B: Are you writing something?
A: Yes, I am, but what?
B: Are you writing a letter?
A: Yes, I am. Now it's your turn.

6 Write down the names of four people in your family. Tell your partner what you think each person is doing at the moment.

I think my brother Alex is probably . . . ing.

7 Look at the painting. In pairs, write five sentences to describe what you can see and what the people are doing. Use a dictionary to help you.

Bank Holiday (William Strang)

8 READING AND LISTENING

You work with Chris and Adam at the travel agent's. Chris is on holiday at the moment and sends you a postcard. Read it and then tell Adam about it.

Listen and answer Adam's questions.

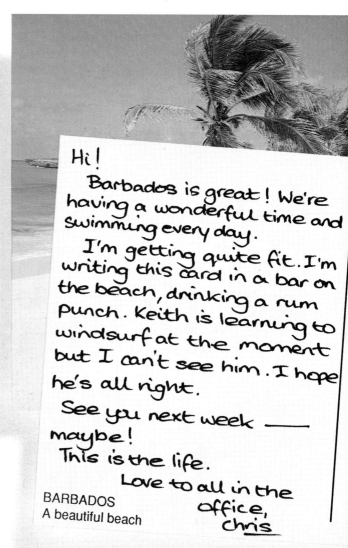

Hi!
Barbados is great! We're having a wonderful time and swimming every day.
I'm getting quite fit. I'm writing this card in a bar on the beach, drinking a rum punch. Keith is learning to windsurf at the moment but I can't see him. I hope he's all right.
See you next week ——— maybe!
This is the life.
Love to all in the office,
Chris

BARBADOS
A beautiful beach

9 WRITING

Choose a place in your country for a holiday. Copy and complete the postcard below and address it to someone in the class.

Hi . . . !
    Here I am in . . . I'm having a/an . . . time.
I'm . . . (say what you're doing). I'm writing this in/on . . . (say where). See you . . . (say when).
    Love, . . .

When she is not dancing, Nina is often busy preparing her shoes.

BORN TO DANCE

This week the great Bolshoi Ballet comes to Britain. HELEN THOMAS talks to one of their new ballerinas, Nina Ananiashvili.

Photographs by Colin Jones.

Nina practising with her 80-year-old teacher, Marina Semyonova.

Nina Ananiashvili is a prima ballerina at the Bolshoi Ballet, the greatest ballet company in the world. She lives with her husband Guya, a diplomat, in a flat in Moscow. The flat is very small. The bedroom and the sitting room are in one room and there is only a very small bathroom and kitchen.

Every morning Guya and Nina have breakfast at half past seven. Then Nina prepares her ballet shoes. She uses three new pairs of ballet shoes for every performance. Nina usually walks to her classes at the theatre. 'I love the city,' she says, 'It opens my eyes.'

But on performance days, she takes a taxi to

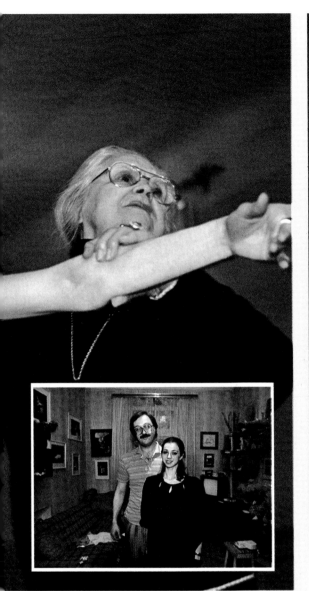

Nina and her husband Guya in their sitting room.

Fluency

UNITS 11–15

1 Before you read

Look at the title of the reading text. What sort of things do you want to know about a ballerina's life?

2 READING

Read the text and say which paragraph is about:

– Nina's morning routine (paragraph 2)
– who Nina is and where she lives
– Nina's routine on performance days
– the rewards of being a ballerina
– what Nina does after a performance

3 ROLEPLAY

Use the cues below to write some of the interviewer's questions. Then roleplay an interview with Nina in pairs.

Where/live/Moscow?
What/flat/like?
What/do/in the morning?
What/do/on performance days?
What/do/after the performance?

Start your roleplay like this:

YOU: Nina, you're a prima ballerina at the Bolshoi Ballet.
NINA: Yes, that's right.
YOU: Where do you live in Moscow?

4 Tell the class three facts in the text which you think are interesting.

5 🔊 LISTENING

Listen and complete the list of furniture there is in Nina and Guya's flat in Moscow.

Sitting room	Kitchen
a sofa	a table
a table	two chairs
an . . .	a . . .
a big . . .	a . . .
a video recorder	
a . . .	
a . . .	

class and back. 'I like to save my energy,' she says. She arrives at the theatre at about five o'clock in the evening. The performance starts at seven thirty.

Dancing is very tiring and some ballerinas lose three kilos during a performance. Nina is always very thirsty after a performance. 'I drink and drink: water, tea, lemonade, anything. Usually I can't sleep until three or four o'clock in the morning.'

Bolshoi dancers earn quite a lot of money and there are other rewards. Girls stand in shopping queues to buy food for her. 'Men just leave flowers outside my flat and then run away!' says Nina, and laughs.

Check

UNITS 11-15

1 Complete the text with the correct form of the present simple of the verbs in brackets.

Gavin Hunter is 32 years old. He is a farmer and (1) (live) *lives* in Somerset with his wife and two children. Every morning he (2) (get up) . . . at 6.00 and (3) (make) . . . tea for his wife, Helen, and (4) (prepare) . . . a bottle of milk for his baby daughter, Kate. At about 6.30 he (5) (milk) . . . the cows and after breakfast he (6) (work) . . . on the farm.

Gavin (7) (have) . . . his main meal of the day at lunchtime. In the evening Gavin and Helen usually (8) (watch) . . . television. They (9) (go) . . . to bed at about 10.30. Last thing at night Gavin (10) (listen to) . . . the weather forecast on the radio.

2 Choose the correct form of the verb.

Example
1 At the moment she has/she is having a shower.
1 At the moment she has/she is having a shower.

1 At the moment she has/she is having a shower.
2 I like/I am liking this music.
3 What do you do/are you doing with that pen?
4 Do you listen/Are you listening to the radio every morning?
5 Do you listen/Are you listening to me?

3 Write the times.

Example
1 8 a.m.
1 *Eight o'clock in the morning.*

1 8 a.m.
2 2 p.m.
3 11 p.m.
4 7 p.m.
5 6 a.m.

4 Use the words in brackets to write the correct question for each answer.

Example
1 (start work)   At 7.30 in the morning.
1 *What time do you start work?*

1 (start work)   At 7.30 in the morning.
2 (get to work)   By car.
3 (journey take)   About three quarters
                      of an hour.
4 (far)   Five kilometres.
5 (park your car)   In the factory car park.
6 (finish work)   At 5 p.m.
7 (get home)   At about quarter to
                      six in the evening.
8 (your wife work)   No, she doesn't.
9 (do after supper)   We watch TV.
10 (go to bed)   At about 11 o'clock.

5 Complete the text with the correct preposition.

at (x2)   from (x2)   in (x2)   on   to (x3)
by   for

Marie-France (1) *from* Saint-Nazaire on the north-west coast of France, works as a secretary (2) *for* an insurance company.

Marie-France works (3) . . . nine o'clock (4) . . . the morning (5) . . . five o'clock (6) . . . the evening. She usually leaves home (7) . . . eight o'clock and goes (8) . . . bus (9) . . . her office.

(10) . . . Monday and Wednesday evenings she goes (11) . . . Italian classes (12) . . . the local college.

6 Rewrite the sentences putting the adverb in the correct place.

Example
1 ALWAYS He has breakfast in bed.
1 *He always has breakfast in bed.*

1 ALWAYS He has breakfast in bed.
2 NEVER She is late for work.
3 SOMETIMES We play cards all night.
4 OFTEN I eat my lunch in the park.
5 USUALLY They are at home on Saturday
           morning.

7 Complete the sentences with the correct form of *there is/are*.

there's (x2)   is there (x2)
there are (x2)   are there (x2)
there is   there isn't

Example
1 . . . a beautiful park near our house.
1 There's a beautiful park near our house.

1 . . . a beautiful park near our house.
2 . . . three people from Kuwait in our class.
3 . . . any good restaurants in this town?
4 A: . . . a coffee machine in this building?
 B: No, . . .
5 . . . some more chairs in the dining room.
6 A: . . . a shower in your hotel room?
 B: Yes, . . .
7 . . . a telephone in the front hall.
8 . . . any interesting people in your class?

8 Complete the sentences with *a, an, the* or – (no article).

Example
1 We live in . . . small house.
1 We live in a small house.

1 We live in . . . small house
2 I love . . . classical music.
3 He plays . . . guitar quite well.
4 She's . . . student at my college.
5 Children start . . . school at five years old in Britain.
6 What time do you get . . . home in . . . evening?
7 On Monday morning I have . . . breakfast at six o'clock.
8 She works in . . . office in . . . centre of town.

9 Put the furniture and fittings into one of the rooms of the house in the table below.

KITCHEN	BATHROOM	BEDROOM	SITTING ROOM
sink			

sink   sofa   television   washbasin
shower   toilet   bed   fridge
dressing table   armchair   bath
cooker   fridge   table   wardrobe

CHECK YOUR PROGRESS

Add up your score. How well did you do?

Easy exercises . . .
Difficult exercises . . .
Problems . . .

LEARNING TO LEARN 3: Recording vocabulary

Learning new words is very important. Here are some ways of recording new words:

1 During the lesson, write important words in your notebook.
2 Later, copy them into a separate vocabulary book.
3 Write a translation or an explanation of each word and an example of how to use it, e.g.
 temperature   'fiebre'   She's got a temperature.
 awful   terrible   The weather is awful.
4 If possible, write words in groups in your vocabulary book, e.g.
 Colours   Rooms   Adjectives
 red   kitchen   big
 green   bathroom   small

Preview

UNITS 16-20

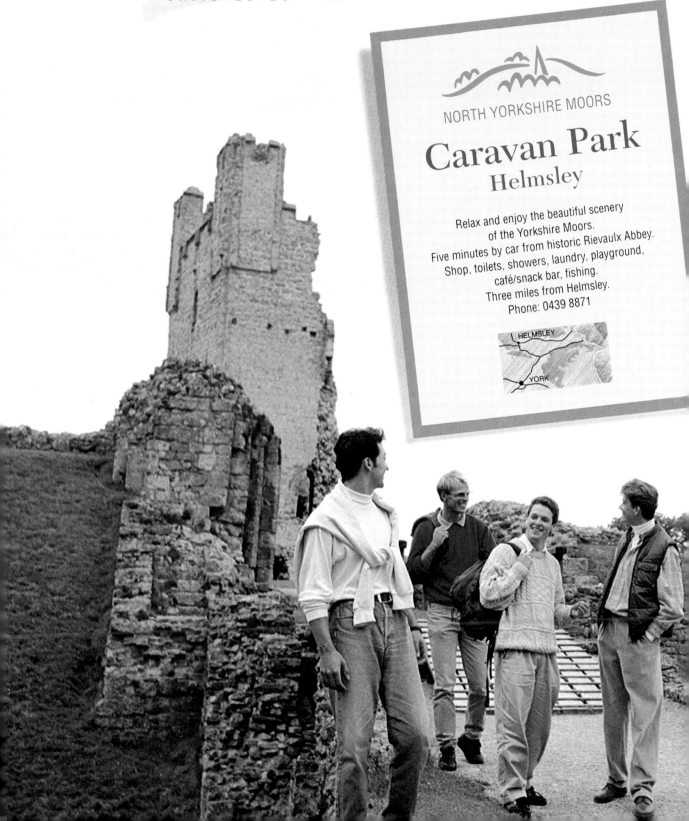

🔊 **Listen and follow the conversations.**

Adam is on a weekend break in the Yorkshire Moors.

NORTH YORKSHIRE MOORS

Caravan Park
Helmsley

Relax and enjoy the beautiful scenery of the Yorkshire Moors.
Five minutes by car from historic Rievaulx Abbey.
Shop, toilets, showers, laundry, playground, café/snack bar, fishing.
Three miles from Helmsley.
Phone: 0439 8871

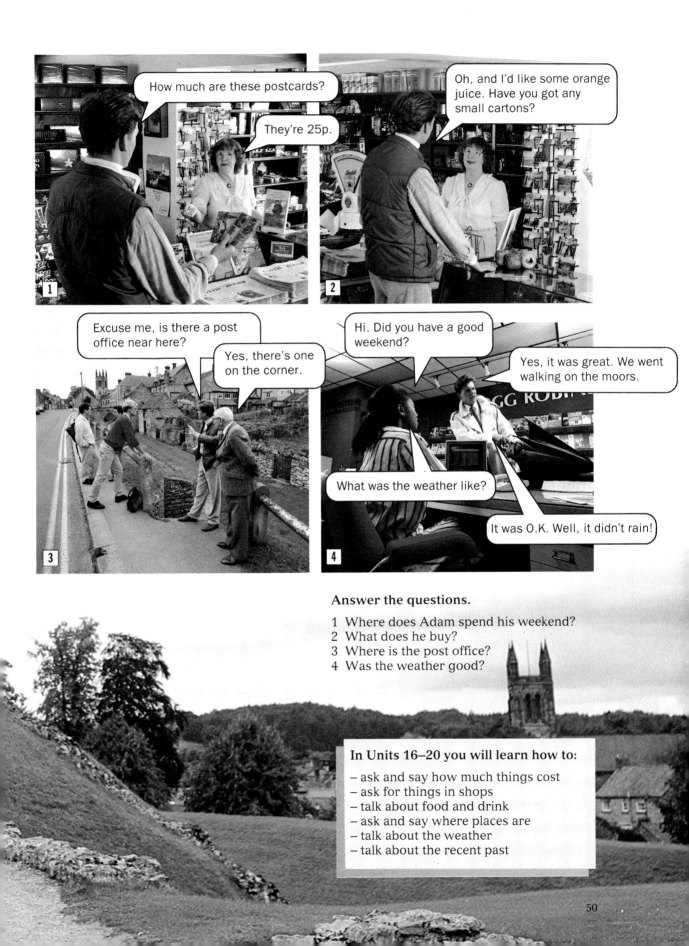

Answer the questions.

1 Where does Adam spend his weekend?
2 What does he buy?
3 Where is the post office?
4 Was the weather good?

In Units 16–20 you will learn how to:

– ask and say how much things cost
– ask for things in shops
– talk about food and drink
– ask and say where places are
– talk about the weather
– talk about the recent past

16
Prices

CUSTOMER: Could I have that box of chocolates, please?
ASSISTANT: Which one?
CUSTOMER: The big one. How much is it?
ASSISTANT: It's £8.99.
CUSTOMER: That's very expensive!

Note
1p = a *penny* or *one p* /piː/
£1 = a *pound* or *one pound*
£5 = *five pounds*
£4.99 = *four (pounds) ninety-nine (pence)*

1 ▣ LISTENING

Listen and write the price of each article. Then note the items which the customer thinks are expensive.

Item	Price	Expensive?
1 a box of chocolates 2 a T-shirt 3 a camera		

COMMUNICATION FOCUS:

Asking for things

Can I have Could I have	a T-shirt, a big one, this/that pen, these/those chocolates,	please?

Asking the price

How much is	it? the T-shirt? this one/that one?	It's £7.99.
How much are	they? the/these/those/chocolates? the large ones?	They're £3.50.

2 Match the words with the correct pictures below.

bottle can packet loaf
tube box carton bar

1 a . . . of tissues

2 a . . . of lemonade

80p £1.20

3 a . . . of crisps

4 a . . . of toothpaste

18p

90p

5 a . . . of chocolate

24p

6 a . . . of mineral water

7 a . . . of milk

 30p

70p

8 a . . . of bread

3 Buy the items above.

A: Can/Could I have a . . ., please?
B: Yes, certainly.
A: How much is it?
B: It's . . .

1 AT A HAMBURGER RESTAURANT
a King-size hamburger	£2.75p	
a portion of chips	small: 50p	large: 70p
a glass of orange juice	65p	
a cup of coffee	55p	

2 AT A BAKER'S
a cheese roll	70p
a ham roll	80p
a packet of sandwiches	£1.25
a fruit tart	85p
a loaf of bread	70p

3 AT A CHEMIST'S
a packet of aspirin	small: 85p	large: £1.90
a box of tissues	80p	
a bottle of antiseptic	small: 99p	large: £1.42
a tube of sun cream	small: £1.75	large: £3.00
a film	£2.10	

4 ROLEPLAY

One of you is the assistant and the other is the customer. Act out conversations in the places above.

ASSISTANT	CUSTOMER
Can I help you?	
	Yes, can/could I have . . ., please?
(A small one or a large one?)	
	(A (large) one, please.)
Yes, anything else?	
	Yes, I'd like . . .
Anything else?	
	No, thank you. How much is that?
That's . . ., please.	

5 In groups, discuss and note down the current prices of these items in your country.

a daily newspaper   25p
a litre of milk   60p
a loaf of bread   70p
a cinema ticket   £3
a pair of jeans   £31.99
a litre of petrol   52p
a cup of coffee   55p
a packet of cigarettes   £1.65
a small family car   £7,000
a night in a three-star hotel   £55

A: How much does a litre of petrol cost?
B: It's about . . .
C: It depends. A litre of leaded petrol costs . . . but a litre of unleaded costs . . .

6 What is £1 (a pound) worth in your currency? Which British prices do you think are cheap and which expensive?

I think . . . for . . . is cheap but . . . . is/are expensive.

17
Food and drink

3 DIALOGUE

Adam shares a flat with his older brother, Michael. Read the dialogue and write down Adam's shopping list.

MICHAEL: Are you going to the shops?

ADAM: Yes, I need some new batteries for my radio.

MICHAEL: Well, we haven't got any eggs or milk. Can you get some?

ADAM: O.K.

MICHAEL: And we need some coffee too.

ADAM: All right. Have you got any money?

MICHAEL: Here's a ten pound note. Oh, and can you get me the *TV Times*?

ADAM: Why can't you go to the shops yourself?

MICHAEL: Because I'm lazy!

1 Find these items in the picture. Which items are not in the picture?

bread	salt	yoghurt	apples
milk	pepper	cheese	oranges
eggs	sugar	chicken	bananas
butter	coffee	oil	potatoes
biscuits	tea	vinegar	tomatoes

2 🔲 SPEECHWORK

Repeat the phrases. Remember to say /ənd/ not /ænd/ each time.

fish and chips	bread and butter
milk and sugar	cheese and biscuits
oil and vinegar	salt and pepper

4 🔲 LISTENING

Listen to a similar conversation and note four differences.

GRAMMAR FOCUS:

Countable nouns	Uncountable nouns
Singular	(some) bread
an egg	(some) milk
Plural	
(some) eggs	

List the items in Exercise 1 in groups of countable and uncountable nouns.

GRAMMAR FOCUS: *Some, any* and *no*

Positive
We need **some** eggs/bread/milk.

Question
Have we got **any** eggs/bread/milk?

Negative
We haven't got **any** eggs/bread/milk.
We've got **no** eggs/bread/milk.

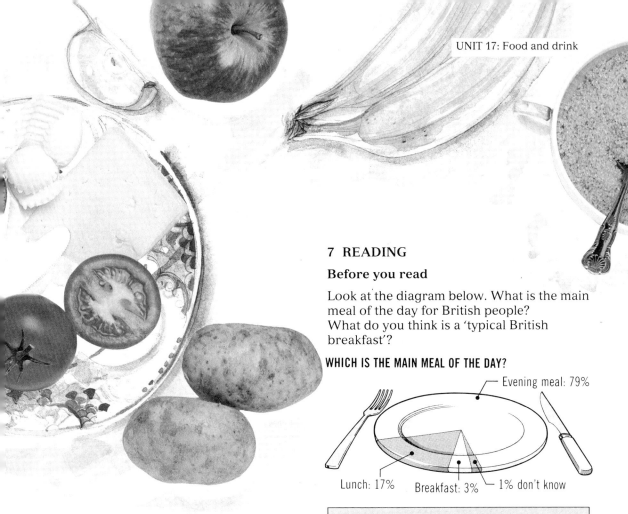

7 READING

Before you read

Look at the diagram below. What is the main meal of the day for British people?
What do you think is a 'typical British breakfast'?

WHICH IS THE MAIN MEAL OF THE DAY?

Evening meal: 79%

Lunch: 17%   Breakfast: 3%   1% don't know

5 ROLEPLAY

You want your partner to do some shopping for you. Make a shopping list of four items. Act out the dialogue.

A: Are you going to the shops?
B: Yes, I am.
A: Well, we haven't got any . . . or . . . Can you get some?
B: O.K. Anything else?
A: Yes, we need some . . .

6 With which country do you associate the following food and drink?

1 chicken curry
2 sweet and sour pork
3 hamburgers
4 spaghetti bolognese
5 sachertorte
6 coffee
7 fish and chips
8 sauerkraut
9 gazpacho
10 bouillabaisse
11 kebabs
12 chilli con carne
13 borscht
14 port

1 India

(Answers are on page 141).

List the words in the following categories.

soups   fish dishes   meat dishes
vegetable dishes   desserts   drinks

ABOUT MEALS IN BRITAIN

According to a recent survey, the main meal of the day for most British people is the evening meal. Seven out of ten families with children sit down at a table for their weekday evening meal, not in front of television, as many people think. For most British families, eating is the main social activity of the day.

But breakfast is different. Only one out of four have breakfast with other members of the family. The survey also reveals that the traditional British cooked breakfast of sausage, bacon, eggs and fried bread is disappearing. Only twelve per cent of the population have a regular cooked breakfast. Most people now prefer cereal or muesli, toast and marmalade and a cup of tea or coffee.

8 About you

1 What is your main meal of the day?
2 When and where do you have it?
3 Are your eating habits different at the weekend?
4 What do you usually have for breakfast?
5 Do you ever have a cooked breakfast?
6 Are your habits typical?

18
Location

GRAMMAR FOCUS:
Prepositions of place

next to	on the corner (of)	over
opposite	on the left (of)	under
between	on the right (of)	inside
behind	in front (of)	outside

1 Make as many sentences as you can about the places and the people in the picture.

There's a taxi outside the supermarket.
The bank is on the corner.

2 ▣ SPEECHWORK

Listen and underline the main stressed syllable.

supermarket   post office   cinema
restaurant   bus stop   taxi rank

3 ACTIVITY

bank	hotel	bus station
post office	theatre	supermarket
car park	cinema	swimming pool

STUDENT A
Draw the basic street map above. Mark the places on the map where you like.

STUDENT B
Draw the basic street map above. Ask questions to find out where the places are on A's map and mark them on your map.

B: Where's the bank?
A: It's in . . . street opposite the . . .

4 ROLEPLAY

One of you is a visitor to your town and wants to do the following things. In pairs, act out a conversation.

buy a guide book   post a parcel
park her/his car   change some travellers'
                 cheques

A: Excuse me. Is there a bookshop near here? I want to buy a guide book.
B: Yes, there's one in . . . next to . . .

5 WRITING

Read the note that Mrs Gibson leaves for a friend. Write a similar note to a visitor who is going to use your home while you are away.

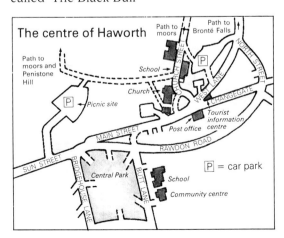

Vicky,
Just a short note to tell you about the local shops. There's a newsagent's on the corner of Heath Road, and just opposite there's a launderette and a chemist's. We use the supermarket next to Lloyds Bank – the one in our street isn't very good.
Enjoy your stay,
Sheila

6 🔊 LISTENING

Laura is in Haworth. Listen and find where the following are.

a) Laura   b) the Brontë Museum   c) the pub called 'The Black Bull'

The centre of Haworth

7 READING

Read and answer the questions.

1 Who were the Brontë sisters?
2 Name three of their novels.
3 What was their brother's job?
4 Where is their house?
5 Where was their favourite walk?
6 What was the setting for the novel *Wuthering Heights*?

The Brontë sisters and their home

The three Brontë sisters were all famous writers. The eldest sister, Charlotte, is famous for *Jane Eyre*, a novel published in 1847; Emily for *Wuthering Heights* and Anne for *The Tenant of Wildfell Hall*. Their brother, Patrick Branwell, was an artist and a railway clerk. All the family died young.

The Brontës' house is at the top of the steep main street of the village of Haworth. It is now a museum. One of the Brontës' favourite walks was across the moors to a waterfall, now called 'The Brontë Waterfall'. You can still see the ruins of an old house high up on the moors, which people say was the setting for *Wuthering Heights*. You can also visit The Black Bull pub in Haworth, where Patrick Branwell Brontë slowly drank himself to death.

48

Weather and seasons

1 Look at the weather map. What's the weather like in the south of England today? Is it warm and dry or cold and wet?

YOUR WEATHER TODAY

Dry and sunny, with some light rain in Scotland and northern parts of England and Wales. Maximum temperature 17°C (62°F)

OUTLOOK:
Remaining warm and sunny but cooler weather will spread across southern England at the weekend.

2 VOCABULARY

Complete the list of weather words.

NOUN	ADJECTIVE	VERB
sun	sunny	the sun is shining
cloud	...	–
rain	...	it's raining
snow	...	it's ...
fog	...	–
wind	...	–

3 📼 LISTENING

Listen and note the weather words and temperatures you hear.

WEATHER REPORT

TODAY'S WEATHER:
cold cool dry raining drizzle

TEMPERATURE (°C):
0 2 4 6 8 10

OUTLOOK FOR TOMORROW:
foggy cloudy sunny windy

TEMPERATURE (°C):
0 2 4 6 8 10

4 Look at the photographs and say what the weather is like in each city.

A: What's the weather like in Mexico City today?
B: It's hot and sunny.

Mexico City

Moscow

London

Tokyo

GRAMMAR FOCUS:
Verb *to be* – past simple

Question	Positive/Negative
What was the weather like?	It was hot. It wasn't cold.
	Short answer
Was it hot?	Yes, it was.
Was it cold?	No, it wasn't.

5 Look at the world weather chart and say what the weather was like in the same cities yesterday.

A: What was the weather like in . . . yesterday?

B: It was . . ./It rained./It snowed.

World Weather

C: cloud, Fg: fog, R: rain, Sn: snow, S: sun

		C	F			C	F			C	F
Amsterdam	S	14	57	Lisbon	R	18	64	Peking	Fg	15	59
Athens	S	17	63	London	Fg	15	59	Rio de Janeiro	S	23	73
Berlin	R	13	55	Luxembourg	C	11	52	Rome	R	17	63
Brussels	C	16	61	Madrid	S	16	61	Stockholm	Sn	2	36
Buenos Aires	C	15	59	Mexico City	S	20	68	Sydney	s	21	70
Cairo	S	22	72	Moscow	Sn	2	36	Tokyo	C	16	62
Geneva	Fg	9	48	New Delhi	S	30	86	Vancouver	C	11	55
Istanbul	R	11	52	Oslo	Sn	4	39	Vienna	Fg	14	57
Lima	S	18	64	Paris	Fg	15	63	Washington	R	19	68

6 Ask and talk about your country's weather today and yesterday.

7 Write the months of the year in the correct order.

March   September   January
December   June   April   November
August   February   May   July   October

Note
Months start with a capital letter.

8 📼 SPEECHWORK

Listen and say the months. Mark the stressed syllable or word each time.

9 READING

Read and answer the questions.

1 When does summer officially start and finish in Britain?
2 Why do people in Britain talk about the weather a lot?
3 How can you start a conversation with a stranger?
4 Which months do you think Lord Byron liked best?

ABOUT THE SEASONS AND WEATHER IN BRITAIN

There are four seasons – spring, summer, autumn and winter. Spring officially starts in March, summer in June, autumn in September and winter in December. But sometimes we have weather from each season all in one day.

Because English weather changes so often, there is always something to talk about. A remark to a stranger about the weather such as: 'Not a very nice day, is it?' can often lead to an interesting conversation.

Even poets talk about the weather. For example, Lord Byron (1788–1824) once said: 'I like the weather, when it is not raining. That is, I like two months of every year.'

10 Answer the questions about the seasons in your country.

1 Which months are the spring/summer/autumn/winter months?
2 When do most people have their main holidays?
3 What seasons or months do you associate with: flowers, falling leaves, Carnival time, family gatherings?

11 WRITING

Write a sentence about each season in your country. Say if you like it or not and why.

I like summer because I like swimming and . . .

VISIT FLORIDA
Coast to coast to coast

Last year over forty-two million people visited Florida. With winter temperatures of 60°F to 70°F and summer temperatures in the 80s, the weather makes it an ideal place for a holiday. And of course, it has world-famous attractions like 'Disneyworld'.

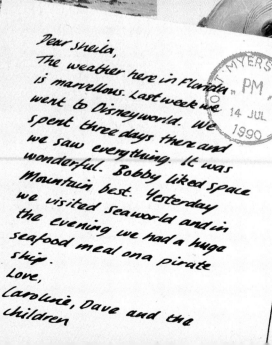

Dear Sheila,
The weather here in Florida is marvellous. Last week we went to Disneyworld. We spent three days there and we saw everything. It was wonderful. Bobby liked Space Mountain best. Yesterday we visited Seaworld and in the evening we had a huge seafood meal on a pirate ship.
Love,
Caroline, Dave and the children

FORT MYERS · FL 339
PM
14 JUL
1990

36 USAirmail
Igor Sikorsky

Mrs S. Gibson,
1, Hull Road,
York,
404 2HT,
England

20
Past events (1)

Before you read

Where do people from your country like to go for their holidays?

1 READING

Read the postcard and say which statements are true.

1 Caroline and her family are on holiday in Florida.
2 They went to Disneyworld last week.
3 They spent two days there.
4 Bobby didn't like Space Mountain.
5 In the evening they had dinner on a ship.

2 Find the past tense forms of the following verbs in the postcard.

have visit is see go spend like

What is the ending of the regular past tense? Which verbs are regular and which are irregular?

3 ▣ SPEECHWORK

Listen and repeat the past tense forms.

talked   liked   walked
stayed   lived   enjoyed
visited   wanted   started

4 Imagine that you are just back from holiday. Use the chart at the bottom of the page to ask and answer about the places you visited. Use these questions.

Where did you go for your
  holiday?
How long did you stay?
What did you do there?
What was the weather like?
And how was the hotel?

5 WRITING

Write a postcard to a friend or relative from a favourite holiday place.

GRAMMAR FOCUS: Past simple

Question	*Positive/Negative*
Where did you go?	We went to Florida.
	We didn't go to Los Angeles.
	Short answer
Did you go to Florida?	Yes, we did.
Did you go to Los Angeles?	No, we didn't.

What word comes before *you* in all the questions?

Rating
✓✓ = great/very good/
        marvellous
✓ = all right/quite good/
        quite nice
✗ = not very good/awful
££ = expensive

HOW WAS YOUR HOLIDAY?

Place:	Brighton	Bali	Biarritz	Barcelona
Length of stay:	2 weeks	10 days	3 weeks	1 week
Activities:	went on an English course	relaxed on the beach	swam and sunbathed	went sightseeing
The weather:	✗	✓✓	✓	✓✓
The hotel:	✓	✓	✗	✓
The food:	££	✓✓	££	✓✓
The beaches:	✗	✓✓	✓✓	

Trip to London

SIGHTSEEING

St Paul's Cathedral

The Houses of Parliament

The Tower of London

WEATHER

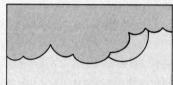

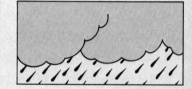

SHOPPING

£5.99

a London bus

£11.99

a Eurythmics CD

£9.50

an apron

SHOPS

TOWER RECORDS

Selfridges

Fluency

UNITS 16–20

1 Yesterday you spent a day and evening in London. Look at the chart on the left and decide where you went, what the weather was like, what you bought and so on.

Example
Sightseeing: The Tower of London
Weather: cloudy
Shopping: Eurythmics CD

2 Find out how your partner spent his/her day in London. Start like this:

A: Did you have a nice time in London?
B: Yes, I did.
A: Did you go sightseeing?
B: Yes, I went to . . .

Use the cues below.

Go/sightseeing?
What/weather like?
Do/any shopping?
What/buy?
How much?
Where exactly is (name of shop or place)?
What/do in the evening?

3 📼 LISTENING

Listen to an Italian woman talking about how she spent some days in London. Did she do any of the things you did?

4 PROJECT and ROLEPLAY

In groups of four or six, plan a similar chart in English for your own town or capital city. Then, in pairs, use the chart to roleplay a conversation with an English-speaking visitor. Find out how the visitor spent his/her day and evening in your city.

5 WRITING

Write a postcard to an English-speaking friend telling him/her about your day in London (or another city). Start like this:

Dear . . .,
I'm writing this from London. I had a
wonderful day yesterday. In the morning I
went to see . . .

EVENING ACTIVITIES

Show

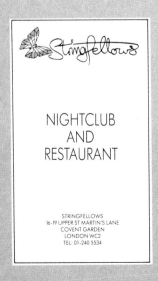

Dancing

Special outing

Check

UNITS 16-20

1 Choose the correct answer.

Example
1 MAN: Can I help you?
  GIRL: Yes, please. . . . some sunglasses.
    a) I like (b) I'd like   c) I have

1 MAN: Can I help you?
  GIRL: Yes, please. . . . some sunglasses.
    a) I like   b) I'd like   c) I have

2 MAN: Yes, of course. . . . sunglasses are all
    under £10.
    a) These   b) This   c) That

3 GIRL: I like the black . . . very much. How
    much are they?
    a) one   b) those   c) ones

  MAN: They're £9.20.

4 GIRL: All right, and . . . a packet of aspirins
    too, please?
    a) could I have   b) have you
    c) I like

5 MAN: That's 45p. Anything . . . ?
    a) all   b) else   c) other

  GIRL: No, thanks. That's all.

2 Rewrite the phrases with the correct words.

Example
1 a tube of bread
1 *a tube of toothpaste*

1 a tube of bread
2 a box of toothpaste
3 a bottle of crisps
4 a loaf of matches
5 a packet of mineral water

3 Answer the questions using *one* or *ones*.

Example
1 Which car do you like? (red)
1 *The red one.*

1 Which car do you like? (red)
2 Which packet do you want? (small)

3 Which biscuits do you want? (chocolate)
4 Which shoes do you like best? (Italian)
5 Which bag do you like? (big)

4 Choose the odd word out.
Example

1 butter milk cheese (spaghetti)

 1 butter milk cheese spaghetti
 2 bread water milk lemonade
 3 salt pepper fish sugar
 4 table chair bathroom wardrobe
 5 bank post office school garden
 6 spring rain summer autumn
 7 sunny rainy winter cloudy
 8 January May Tuesday July
 9 cup milk glass bottle
10 yesterday last week
   tomorrow last weekend

5 Write if the nouns are countable (C) or uncountable (UC).

Example
1 *banana C*

1 banana   6 bread
2 milk   7 apple
3 vegetable   8 meat
4 oil   9 hamburger
5 egg   10 coffee

6 Complete the dialogue with *some, any* or *no*.

MICHAEL: Adam, have we got (1) *any* eggs?
ADAM: No, I don't think so.
MICHAEL: Look in the fridge.
ADAM: No, there are (2) . . . eggs here.
MICHAEL: What about milk?
ADAM: No, we haven't got (3) . . . milk. We
       finished it last night.
MICHAEL: And I suppose we haven't got (4)
       . . . sugar either!
ADAM: What do you want to make?
MICHAEL: I want to make (5) . . . cakes!
ADAM: Well, you can't! Have another cup
       of tea and a biscuit.

7 Where are they sitting? Look at the diagram of the class and complete the sentences using the correct preposition.

behind   in front of   next to   opposite
between

Example
1 Paul is sitting . . . Ben.
1 Paul is sitting next to Ben.

1 Paul is sitting . . . Ben.
2 Kate is sitting . . . Bill and Emma.
3 Sam, Jill and Tom are sitting . . . Sue, Paul and Ben.
4 Tom is sitting . . . Emma.
5 The teacher is sitting . . . the class.

8 Complete the phrases with *in, on* or *at*.

Example
1 . . . December
1 In December

1 . . . December	6 . . . the evening
2 . . . Monday	7 . . . July
3 . . . spring	8 . . . Tuesday afternoon
4 . . . autumn	9 . . . the weekend
5 . . . midnight	10 . . . the morning

9 Match a word from the left-hand column with a word from the right-hand column to make a building or place.

1 super
1 supermarket

1 super	a) pool
2 post	b) bar
3 bus	c) market
4 taxi	d) shop
5 swimming	e) rank
6 car	f) office
7 news	g) agent
8 book	h) stop
9 snack	i) park

10 Sue is on holiday. Use the notes to write sentences about how she spent her day yesterday.

Example
1 – get up at 8 o'clock
1 She got up at 8 o'clock.

1 – get up at 8 'clock
2 – go for a swim before breakfast
3 – spend the morning on the beach
4 – have lunch at a beach café
5 – swim and sunbathe in the afternoon
6 – have a windsurfing lesson at 4 p.m.
7 – relax in the hotel
8 – have a drink in the bar
9 – go to a restaurant in town
10 – go dancing at a disco

CHECK YOUR PROGRESS

Add up your score. How well did you do?

Easy exercises . . .
Difficult exercises . . .
Problems . . .

LEARNING TO LEARN 4: Learning vocabulary

Here are some tips for learning new words:

1 Copy the new words into a vocabulary book. (*See Learning to learn 3*)
2 Say the words several times, silently or aloud.
3 Think about each word as you say it. Try to make a picture of the word in your mind, e.g. *horse.*
4 Try to make an association, e.g.
   cousin: think of one of your cousins
   beach: think of a beach you like.

Find out the meaning of these words. Learn them using the ways suggested above.
1 opposite 2 petrol 3 chemist 4 lucky 5 lazy 6 corner 7 fog 8 season

Preview

🔲 Listen and follow the conversations.

The one looking at you. She's wearing a white skirt.

Oh, it's Laura.

3

What are you going to do?

I'm going to say hello!

4

Hello, Laura. Why didn't you return my phone calls?

I'm sorry, Adam. I was really busy.

5

Is this your car? It's very nice.

Er no . . . It isn't mine. It's my brother's. Look, let's go for a coffee.

Answer the questions.

1 Who is Adam with?
2 Who is Laura with?
3 Why didn't Laura phone Adam?
4 Is the car Adam's?
5 Where are they going now?

In Units 21–25 you will learn how to:

– talk about personal property
– describe clothes
– talk about future plans
– make suggestions
– describe appearance
– talk about past events in sequence

Is this yours?

Heavens, yes! Thanks. Where did you find it?

You left it in the bank.

Whose is the yellow car on the other side of the road?

It's mine.

Well, you've got a parking ticket, I'm afraid!

21
Personal property

1 Look at the photographs and answer the questions.

1 What did the woman leave in the bank?
2 Why is the waiter pointing at the yellow car?

2 Exchange possessions with other students in the class. Then say who the possessions belong to.

A: Whose bag is this?
B: It's mine./It's Julio's.

3 In pairs, look at the pictures below and use the pronouns in the Focus box to say who each thing belongs to.

A: Whose is the Volvo?
B: I think it's his./it's the man's.

WHO DOES IT REALLY BELONG TO?

HAVE YOUR GOT A/AN ... IN YOUR HOME ?	YES/NO	IS IT YOURS?	IF NOT, WHOSE IS IT?
stereo system			
cassette recorder			
home computer			
atlas			
bible			
pet (dog, cat, bird)			
piano			
sewing machine			
electric drill			
alarm clock			

4 In pairs, complete the questionnaire for yourself and your partner.

A: Have you got a stereo system in your home?
B: Yes, I/we have.
A: Is it yours?
B: No, it isn't. It's my sister's.

5 ▭ SPEECHWORK

Which word in each line does not rhyme with the other two?

1	yours	doors	ours
2	not	what	cat
3	mine	win	white
4	whose	who's	how's
5	here	her	were

Now listen and see if you were right.

6 ▭ LISTENING

Listen to this conversation at a leisure centre. Complete the information below.

LOST
Item(s): _____
Description: _____
Where left or lost: _____
When: _____

Now listen again and note down the questions the man asked.

7 WRITING

Imagine that you lose a valuable possession, e.g. a ring, a watch, or an address book. Write a form like the one below on to a piece of paper.

LOST
Item(s): A watch
Description: Gold, with a black strap
Where left or lost: In sports centre
When: On Monday 21st January

8 ROLEPLAY

Distribute the 'forms' around the class so that nobody knows whose they have got. In turn, say what you have found. The owner must prove that it belongs to him/her by answering your questions correctly. Use the questions from Exercise 6 to help you.

A: I've found a watch. Whose is it?
B: I think it's mine.
A: What . . .?
B: . . .
A: O.K. It's yours./No, it isn't yours.

22 Clothes

1 Find these clothes in the picture below. Which clothes can't you find?

a hat	a blazer	a suit	a vest	a tie
a skirt	trousers	a scarf	a tracksuit	boots
a dress	jeans	a blouse	a cardigan	tights
shorts	shoes	a T-shirt	a shirt	a swimsuit
a coat	trainers	a sweater	a raincoat	
an anorak	socks	stockings	a jacket	

2 Can you find any of these patterns and shades in the picture? Point to a person and say what he/she is wearing.

plain   spotted   striped   light (blue)

checked   flowery   patterned   dark (blue)

She's wearing a black and white checked jacket and white skirt.

3 SPEECHWORK

Listen and repeat the words beginning with the sounds /dʒ/ and /j/

jeans jacket jumper John
yellow your yesterday
university

I like your yellow jacket.
I bought some jeans
  yesterday.

4 In pairs, close your eyes and describe the clothes your partner is wearing.

5 About you

1 What style of clothes do you like: casual, smart, old, American, Italian?
2 Where do you buy most of your clothes?
3 Which fashion magazines do you read, if any?

6 🔲 LISTENING

Before you listen

What sort of clothes do students in your country wear?

Listen to a British student talking about his clothes and complete the information.

Today's fashion is customised!

Name: Henry Bourne
Occupation:
Monthly clothes budget:
Favourite style of clothes:
Today's outfit:

7 Make a similar chart and interview someone in the class. Prepare your questions first. Ask questions like this:

How much do you spend a month on clothes?

8 READING

Read the article and circle the correct answers below.

WHAT TO WEAR ON TV

Lisa Aziz, news presenter for the breakfast television programme, TV-am, talks about the clothes she wears for TV.

'Bright, warm colours like yellow and red are more cheerful early in the morning. I don't usually wear dark colours like black or navy blue.

There are also technical problems with some patterns and colours. For example, I can't wear striped, checked or white clothes on TV because they blur. Plain clothes are best.

All TV presenters get a clothes budget and I have a lot of jackets in different colours. We try to wear a different outfit every day.

I present the news behind a desk, so people can only see my top half. I quite often read the news in a smart jacket and jeans!

I don't wear a lot of jewellery on television because I am allergic to most of it. I also think jewellery distracts the viewer from the news.'

1 Which of these colours looks cheerful?
a) navy blue   b) dark green   c) orange

2 Which of these looks best on TV?
a) a striped blouse   b) a plain blouse   c) a checked blouse

3 What sort of clothes does Lisa wear on TV?
a) jackets   b) dresses   c) sweaters

4 Why doesn't she wear a lot of jewellery?
a) It's too expensive.   b) It distracts the viewer.
c) It doesn't suit her.

9 In groups, decide who you think are the world's ten best-dressed people.

10 WRITING

Write a paragraph about yourself and your clothes. Use the headings in Exercise 6.

What are you going to do for your birthday?

I'm going to have a big party.

When are you going to stop smoking?

Next week.

I've got a job interview tomorrow.

What are you going to wear?

A suit.

23
Future plans

1 Answer the questions.

1 What is the girl going to do for her birthday?
2 When is the woman going to stop smoking?
3 What is the woman going to wear for her job interview?

GRAMMAR FOCUS: The *going to* future

The *going to* future is used to talk about what you plan or intend to do in the future.

Question	*Positive*	*Negative*
What are you going to do?	I'm going to have a party.	I'm not going to have a party.
	Short answer	*Short answer*
Are you going to have a party?	Yes, I am.	No, I'm not.

What's the difference in meaning?
1 I get up at 7 o'clock.
2 I'm going to get up at 7 o'clock.

2 ▭ SPEECHWORK

Listen and underline the stressed syllables. Then listen and repeat.

<u>What</u> are you <u>going</u> to <u>do</u>?
What am I going to wear?
When are they going to leave?

3 Find out what your partner is going to do:

– after the lesson   – at the weekend
– this evening   – next summer

4 Decide what to do in these situations.

You often get headaches.
'I'm going to see a doctor.'

1 You didn't sleep well last night.
2 You smoke too much.
3 You do not like your job.
4 You have nothing to wear for an important interview.
5 You get a job in Madrid. You are not Spanish.

5 You are going on a trip to Moscow in January. You can only pack fifteen items of clothing (excluding underwear and socks). Note what you are going to take and decide on two things you are going to buy in Moscow.

Compare lists with your partner and find out if he/she is going to take or buy the same things as you.

A: What are you going to take/buy?
B: I'm going to take two sweaters, . . .

6 ▣ LISTENING

Some tourists are lost in Moscow. They are discussing what to do. Which of these suggestions do they make?

Do they suggest:
asking a policeman?　buying a map?
asking a passer-by?　going to the tourist
asking a tourist?　　office?

COMMUNICATION FOCUS:
Suggestions

Making suggestions	Agreeing
What about asking that woman?	That's a good idea.
	Disagreeing
Let's ask that woman.	No, she can't speak English.

---

7 Plan an International Evening for some visitors to your school. Make suggestions for the evening, using the Focus box and the ideas below to start your discussion.

show slides　　　　　give a talk
sing folk songs　　　put up some posters
show some handicrafts　give a concert

Now tell the other groups what you are going to do. Which ideas were best?

8 READING AND WRITING

Read the note below. Write a similar note to someone in your class explaining your plans for the International Evening and asking him/her to do something for you.

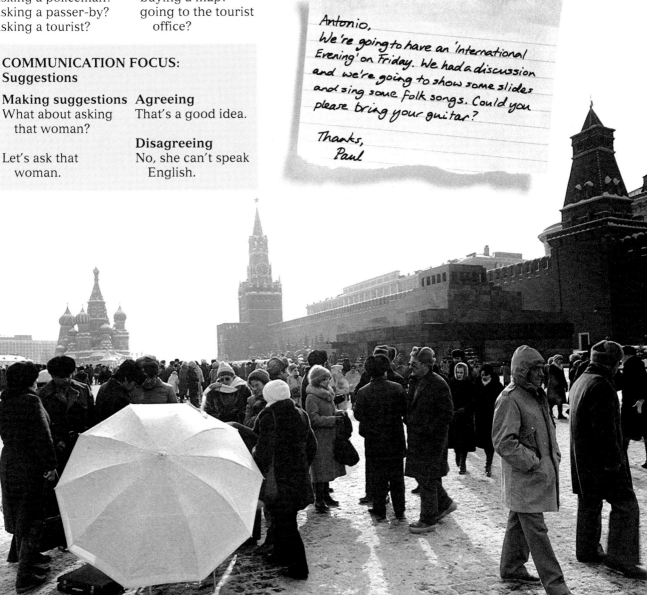

> Antonio,
> We're going to have an 'International Evening' on Friday. We had a discussion and we're going to show some slides and sing some folk songs. Could you please bring your guitar?
>
> Thanks,
> Paul

What's Laura like?

I think Adam's really good-looking.

She's tall, with dark hair. She's really nice.

Mm, he's O.K. but nothing special.

24
Personal appearance

1 In pairs, choose words from the chart to describe Adam.

General appearance:	fair dark pretty good-looking handsome plain ugly
Height:	tall medium-height short
Size:	big small fat thin slim
Hair colour:	blonde fair dark red grey brown
Hair style:	short long straight wavy curly
Eyes:	blue brown grey green
Other features:	beard moustache glasses

2 Find pairs of 'opposite' adjectives in Exercise 1.

tall – short

3 ▭ LISTENING

Look at the pictures below. Listen and say which two people the speakers are describing.

Whitney Houston

Rob Lowe

Michael J. Fox

Gloria Estefan

COMMUNICATION FOCUS:
Describing people

What's she like?	She's tall. She's very friendly.
What does she look like?	She's quite pretty.
What colour/What sort of hair has she got?	She's got long, dark curly hair.
Does she wear glasses?	No, she doesn't.

Note
What's she like? can refer to personality as well as appearance.

4 SPEECHWORK

Practise asking these questions. Try to join the sounds together.

What's she like?
What's he like?
What does she look like?
What does he look like?

5 Ask your partner to describe a friend or relative using the headings in Exercise 1.

A: What's your brother like?
B: He's very good-looking. He's quite tall.

6 WRITING

You are going to stay with an English-speaking family. Complete the letter below with a brief description of yourself.

(Your address)
(Today's date)

Dear Mr and Mrs Castle,

Thank you very much for offering to meet me at the station.

I am . . . (describe your appearance) *and . . .* (give any other details). *I will be wearing . . .* (describe your clothes).

Looking forward to seeing you,
Yours sincerely,

. . .

(Your name)

7 READING

Read how different children describe their fathers. Which of the following features do all the children notice about their fathers?

eyes   hair   job   size/height   age

'I like the way my dad coughs'

They may not know how tall their fathers are but children still have plenty of things to say about their dads!

John-Paul 8
He's big and he's got quite curly hair which stands up. He's clever and he's got quite a lot of money. I like the way he coughs. He doesn't smoke but he coughs quite grown-uply. He's thirty four.

Camilla 8
My daddy's got blue eyes and light brown hair, like me. He's quite handsome and he's quite tall. He lifts me up and throws me in the air. Once he tried to catch me but he missed. I bumped my head.

Hayley 7
He looks nice with black hair. He's very tall and kind. I like helping him wash my mum's car. And I like helping him dry the dishes.

Aisling 7
He's got grey hair and he's fifty years old. He's looking after me while my mum's in hospital. When we were in Ireland on holiday, he let me cross the road on my own.

Past events (2)

1 Say what is happening in each of the pictures. Use these words:

train compartment lock unlock door shout bang conductor

This is not the end of the story. How do you think it ends?

2 Rearrange the sentences to tell the whole story. Start with C.

A When I tried to open the door, I couldn't. I banged and shouted. Soon a conductor heard me and opened the door with a special key.

B I locked the door, got undressed and got into bed. I read a little and then fell asleep.

C I had a ticket for the night train from London to Inverness, in Scotland.

D I said: 'There's something wrong with the lock.' He said: 'No, there isn't. I'll show you.' He came inside and locked the door. 'This is how it works,' he said.

E I woke up at two in the morning because I wanted a drink of water.

F I got on the train and went straight to my compartment.

G We both spent the next three hours locked inside the compartment waiting for someone to let us out.

3 Close your books and tell the story to the class in your own words.

75

4 Find out about the last long journey which your partner made. Ask:

When/last make a long
  journey?
Where/go?
Who/go with?
How/travel?
What time/leave?
Where/have meals?
Sleep on the journey?
Anything happen?
How long/journey take?
Enjoy journey?

A: When did you last make a
   long journey?
B: Last summer.

5 WRITING

Write about your partner's journey. Write three paragraphs starting like this:

PARAGRAPH 1: *Leaving*
He/She/They got up at . . . in
the morning and . . .

PARAGRAPH 2: *The journey*
He/She/They stopped . . .

PARAGRAPH 3: *Arriving*
He/She/They arrived at . . .
and . . .

Link your sentences with *then, and then* and *after* (e.g. *after breakfast*).

6 ▣ LISTENING

Listen to a story about a traveller and say why it is amusing.

7 READING

Before you read

Who was James Dean?
How did he die?
Which films did he make?

Sir Alec Guinness is a famous British actor. In his autobiography, he tells the strange story of the night he met James Dean, a sensational new Hollywood film star.

'In the autumn of 1955 I went to Hollywood to make a film. I arrived after a sixteen-hour journey from Copenhagen and was very tired. I went with a friend to a popular Italian restaurant but unfortunately it was full. As we walked back to the car, I heard someone call my name. I turned and saw a fair-haired young man in a sweatshirt and blue jeans. "Do you want a table?" he asked. "Please join me." The young man was James Dean.

We turned back and he said: "But first I'd like to show you something." In front of the restaurant there was a large, shiny silver sports car tied with a ribbon. There was a bunch of red roses on it. "I've just got it!" he said. "How fast does it go?" I asked. "About 150 miles an hour," he replied.

Suddenly I spoke in a voice that was strange to me: "Don't drive that car. If you do, you will be dead this time next week." James Dean just laughed. I apologised and said I was hungry and tired. We went into the restaurant and had a very enjoyable time. We said goodbye an hour later. We didn't say anything more about the sports car.

At four o'clock the next Friday afternoon, James Dean was dead. He crashed his new sports car on the way to a car rally and died instantly.'

*James Dean made only three films: **East of Eden, Rebel Without a Cause** and **Giant.***

Answer the questions.

1 How long did Alec Guinness's journey to
   Hollywood take?
2 Where did he and his friend go to eat?
3 Where did they meet James Dean?
4 What did he show them?
5 What happened a week later?

rom

ack

n had a £3,000 fur
and taken yesterday
nimal rights activists
ncer.

ne astonished 27-year-old and
was nose to nose with her.
y left her absolutely petrified.'

spokesman added: 'There is a
group of animal rights
ists in Surrey, many of whom
middle class women, and we
ve someone must know who
are. This is the sort of action
I am sure mainstream
sts would condemn
ately. I believe they could
s.

looks like the work of a
group. It was an
nate coincidence that this
picked them out."

f the attackers was about
4in with well groomed
r-length grey hair.
was in her late 20s, 5ft
with straight dark hair
spiky fringe. She was
dark jacket. The third
curly, sandy hair.

cabin staff tied him up to stop him upsetting other passengers. After the plane landed, he was arrested and later appeared at Uxbridge magistrates court, still

drunk too much. 'It is nothing more than a young man from America having been six months in Saudi Arabia without drinks,' he added.

INTERPOL MURDER HUNT COMES TO BRITAIN

By REG EVANS

OFFICERS IN the international police organisation Interpol want to question Jean-Michel Bellingcourt, aged 45, from Louvain in Belgium, about the murder last week of a Dutch couple in a camping site outside Montpellier, France.

French police believe that Mr Bellingcourt caught the boat on Friday from Le Havre in France to Portsmouth.

Police describe the man as about 1.85m tall, thin, with wavy black hair and a moustache. He is wearing jeans, a red T-shirt and a black anorak.

Turn to page 7, Col 6.

1 READING

Read the article and answer the questions.

1 Who are Interpol looking for?
2 Why are they looking for him? (Because they think he murdered . . .)
3 How old is he?
4 How and when did he probably get to Britain?

2 Which of these men looks like Jean-Michel Bellingcourt?

WANTED FOR QUESTIONING

Hampshire Police

WANTED FOR QUESTIONING

Hampshire Police

WANTED FOR QUESTIONING

Hampshire Police

3 ROLEPLAY

Roleplay a conversation with a policeman. Prepare what you are going to say first.

STUDENT A (You)
You are staying at the Seaview Hotel, a small hotel in Portsmouth. You can see the hotel car park from your window. You can see a man looking inside a car. He looks like the Belgian man, Mr Bellingcourt. Telephone the police and say why you are phoning, what the man looks like, what he is wearing and what he is doing. Say what you think he is going to do.

STUDENT B (Policeman)
You are in the police station when someone telephones you. Find out why the person is phoning. Ask questions to complete the information on your form.

Use these cues:

Describe him?
What/wearing?
Where?
What/doing?
Your name and address?

Form 546 (A)

Hampshire Police

Description

sex: .... height: .... size/build: ....

age: .... hair: .... eyes: ....

other features: ....

clothes: ....

Place: ....
Circumstances: ....
....
....
Caller's name: ....
Caller's address: ....
....

Start like this:

B: Hello, Hampshire Police. Can I help you?
A: Yes, I'm staying in a hotel in Portsmouth and I think I can see the man who Interpol are looking for.
B: Can you describe him?

4 ▣ LISTENING

Listen to a news report and answer the question.

Was the man in the car park Mr Bellingcourt?

Check

UNITS 21-25

1 Complete the sentences with the correct question word.

Who Why When (x2) What (x2) Where
Whose How (x2)

Example
1 . . .'s that man over there with the beard?
1 *Who's that man over there with the beard?*

1 . . .'s that man over there with beard?
2 A: . . . can you come and stay for the weekend?
  B: Next month, possibly.
3 . . . long does it take you to get to work in the morning?
4 A: . . . can I buy some fresh milk?
  B: At the shop on the corner.
5 . . .'s your new boss like?
6 . . . keys are these? I found them on the floor.
7 A: . . . do you like living in York?
  B: Because the people are very friendly here.
8 . . . much is that large box of chocolates?
9 . . .'s the name of the travel agent's in the High Street?
10 A: . . . did she move to Manchester?
  B: Last year.

2 Complete the telephone conversation with the correct possessive pronoun.

yours his hers mine theirs

PAT: Mike, I need to borrow a car this weekend.
MIKE: What's wrong with (1) *yours*?
PAT: It's at the garage.
MIKE: I'm sorry but I'm using (2) . . . this weekend.
PAT: Is Sally using (3) . . ., do you know?
MIKE: Yes, she is, I'm afraid. But why not ask John? He doesn't use (4) . . . very often.
PAT: That's a good idea.
MIKE: Or ask the Carters. They only use (5) . . . on Sundays.

3 Write the past tense of the verbs.

Example
1 get got

1 get   6 spend
2 read   7 wake
3 fall   8 come
4 hear   9 say
5 can   10 go

4 Complete each conversation with a question in the past tense.

Example
1 A: I watched a terrible film last night on TV.
  B: What . . .?
1 *What did you watch?*

1 A: I watched a terrible film last night on TV.
  B: What . . .?
2 A: I saw something strange in my garden yesterday.
  B: What . . . ?
3 A: I read some very good books on holiday.
  B: What . . .?
4 A: We went sightseeing yesterday.
  B: Where . . .?
5 A: I bought a present for my sister today.
  B: What . . .?

5 Complete the sentences with the correct form of *going to*.

Example
1 When (you) . . . phone her?
1 *When are you going to phone her?*

1 When (you) . . . phone her?
2 (I not) . . . stay long.
3 (you) . . . play tennis tomorrow?
4 (They) . . . live in Paris for a year.
5 (He not) . . . come to our party.
6 (We) . . . buy a new sofa for the sitting room.
7 Where (you) . . . stay in Luxembourg?
8 What film (she) . . . see?
9 (I not) . . . tell you. It's a secret.
10 (you) . . . have lunch now?

6 Choose the correct words to complete the text.

Sue Lawson is a solicitor in London. She is quite (1) . . . with dark (2) . . . She always wears smart clothes to work. For example, she often wears a (3) . . ., or a blouse and (4) . . . At home she wears casual clothes, like (5) . . . 'I like to be comfortable at the weekends,' she says.

1 a) medium   (b) tall   c) long
2 a) hairs   b) hair   c) eye
3 a) coat   b) suit   c) trousers
4 a) skirt   b) shirt   c) dress
5 a) suit   b) jeans   c) dress

7 Rewrite the sentences putting apostrophes where necessary.

Example
1 The weather wasnt very nice for our holiday.
1 The weather wasn't very nice for our holiday.

1 The weather wasnt very nice for our holiday.
2 Whats the name of Johns doctor?
3 Whos going to sit next to Pam?
4 I didnt see the last James Bond film.
5 Lets ask the boy with the dark hair.
6 Why didnt you answer my letter?
7 Could you sit down? I cant see.
8 That isnt yours. Its mine.
9 She doesnt like wearing dresses.

8 Find twelve words for clothes in the square. You can go across and down.

B	T	H	S	W	E	A	T	E	R
O	I	A	J	E	A	N	S	E	A
O	E	C	I	Z	B	T	Y	N	I
T	M	K	D	T	H	I	O	T	N
S	C	A	R	D	I	G	A	N	C
V	W	I	E	D	U	H	L	F	O
E	H	G	S	U	I	T	P	Q	A
S	K	Y	S	R	O	S	B	V	T
T	J	A	C	K	E	T	M	X	A
G	H	F	U	B	L	O	U	S	E

CHECK YOUR PROGRESS

Add up your score. How well did you do?

Easy exercises . . .
Difficult exercises . . .
Problems . . .

LEARNING TO LEARN 5: Learning grammar

Grammar rules in grammar books are often difficult to understand.
But you can discover grammar rules for yourself:

1 Look at some examples of the grammatical point you are learning.
2 Think about the rule.
3 Look at some examples to see if the rule is right.
4 If not, change the rule.

Remember! You will learn a rule better if you discover it yourself.

Look at these examples of how to form the comparative. What is the rule?
tall – taller   old – older   white – whiter

Now look at these examples.
big – bigger   interesting – more interesting

Do you want to change the rule?

Preview

UNITS 26-30

📇 Listen and follow the conversations.

Hello, Laura speaking.

It's Adam here. Would you like to go to the theatre on Friday?

Yes, I'd love to.

Answer *True* or *False*.

1 Adam invites Laura to go to the cinema.
2 Laura is busy on Friday evening.
3 The play is a comedy.
4 Laura enjoyed the play.

In Units 26–30 you will learn how to:

– talk about dates
– invite people to do things
– talk about definite arrangements
– talk on the telephone
– compare people and places
– talk about temporary activities

26 *Dates and arrangements*

1 🔲 Listen and say the numbers.

Ordinal numbers

1st first	11th eleventh
2nd second	12th twelfth
3rd third	16th sixteenth
4th fourth	20th twentieth
5th fifth	21st twenty-first
6th sixth	30th thirtieth

Dates

You write dates like this:
2nd January, 1991   January 2nd 1991
2/1/91   2.1.91   2 Jan 1991

You say dates like this:
The second of January, nineteen ninety-one.
January the second, nineteen ninety-one.

2 What dates does the Fiesta start and finish?

3 Say the dates.

1/4/1938   15th May   February 2nd
15.11.79   17th June 1990   21st Oct 1988
March 22nd   July 23rd 1992

4 Answer the questions.
1 What's the date today/tomorrow?
2 When is your birthday?
3 When is Bastille Day, May Day, Christmas Day, New Year's Eve?

GRAMMAR FOCUS:
Present continuous (Future use)

Look at these two sentences. Are they about present or future time?

1 What are you doing next weekend?
2 Are you doing anything on 8th July?

Can you use a present tense to talk about future time in your language?

Note
The present continuous tense is used to talk about definite arrangements in the future. It occurs with a time expression, e.g. *this evening, tomorrow, on 21st January.*

5 Find out about some definite arrangements of three students in your class. Tell the class about their arrangements.

Andrea's having a party on Saturday.

6 ▣ LISTENING

Listen to a conversation between Adam and a customer about a trip to Germany. Note down the travel details.

> Date and time of departure:
> Flight number:
> Leaving from:
> Arriving at:
> Arrival time:

7 WRITING

Complete Carole Thompson's letter to her friend, Hanna, in Germany. Date the letter and include the travel details.

23 Park Street
York YO1 5AT
(Date)

Dear Hanna,

I have now got the details of my trip to Frankfurt. I'm . . . .
. . . . .

Thank you for offering to meet me. I'm looking forward to seeing you and Stefan soon.

Love,
Carole

COMMUNICATION FOCUS:
Invitations

Inviting
Would you like to come?

Accepting
Yes, I'd love to.
Yes, that would be great.

Refusing
I'm sorry, I can't.
I'm doing something that day, I'm afraid.

8 ROLEPLAY

STUDENT A
You want to go to see the comedian Lenny Henry and you want Student B to go with you. Saturday is the best night for you, then Friday, then Wednesday. You are not free on Tuesday. Find an evening when Student B is free and arrange to meet.

STUDENT B
Student A wants to invite you to a comedy show next week. This is your diary.

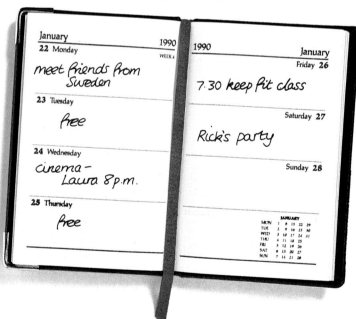

A: Lenny Henry is doing a show next week. Would you like to come?
B: I'd love to, but I'm quite busy next week.
A: Well, what about Saturday the 27th? Are you doing anything that evening?

End your conversation:
A: O.K. I'll get tickets for . . . and I'll meet you outside the theatre at . . .

27
Telephoning

1 🔲 LISTENING

Listen and complete the conversation.

MRS GIBSON: Hello. . . .
ADAM: Oh hello, Mrs Gibson. . . . Adam . . . . . . Laura?
MRS GIBSON: I'm afraid . . .
ADAM: Oh, that's a nuisance.
MRS GIBSON: . . . a message?
ADAM: No, thanks. Just tell her I phoned and I'll . . . later.
MRS GIBSON: O.K. I'll do that. Bye for now.
ADAM: Bye.

COMMUNICATION FOCUS:
Talking on the telephone

Saying your name
This is/It's Adam here.
This is/It's Adam speaking.
(**not** I am Adam speaking.)

Asking for somebody
Can I speak to Laura? (**not** speak with)
Is Laura there/in?

Taking/leaving messages
Can I/you take a message?
Can I leave a message?

Making decisions
I'll call back later.

---

2 🔲 SPEECHWORK

Listen and say if the voice goes up or down at the end of these sentences.

Hello? This is Helen speaking. I'm afraid he's out. It's Laura here. I'll call back later. Who's speaking?

Practise saying the sentences in the same way.

3 Practise telephone conversations with your partner.

CALL 1
You telephone and ask to speak to John. He is out. You do not want to leave a message but will call back later.

CALL 2
You telephone your partner. Your partner answers the phone. You want to know if he/she is doing anything on Saturday morning because you would like him/her to come swimming with you. Say when and where to meet.

Talking Telephones

Ten years ago, people had one telephone in the house and one in the office. Today, people have telephones everywhere: in the house, in the car, in the garden. You even see people walking round the streets with cordless telephones. One man, when recently asked what his telephone number was, answered: 'Which number do you want? My home number, my work number, my weekend number or my car number?'!

4 READING

Before you read

What is unusual about the telephones in the photographs below?

Read the text and answer the questions.

1 Where do people have telephones nowadays?
2 How many telephone numbers did the man have?
3 Why don't people like answerphones?
4 What's wrong with some of the messages which owners put on their machines?

Another new thing is the answerphone. Nobody likes answerphones. For callers there is the problem of how to speak to it. It is very difficult to have a conversation with a machine. Owners of answerphones have problems too. What sort of message do they record?

Some are too short, so the caller doesn't have time to think, for example: 'This is a machine. Speak now.' Others are too long. A New Yorker put a message on his machine which said: 'This is Nathan's answerphone. Please leave your name, number, address, height, weight, qualifications, identity card number and mother's first name. Speak now'! Not surprisingly, people soon stopped telephoning Nathan.

5 About you

1 Have you got a cordless telephone?
2 What do you think of telephones in cars?
3 Do you like leaving messages on answerphones?

6 ▣ LISTENING AND WRITING

Listen and write down the details of the recorded message.

To: From: Time: Message: Caller's phone number:

7 You telephone Jane and Dave but they are out. You want to leave a message on the answerphone. Choose one of the messages below and prepare it.

MESSAGE 1
You want to speak to Jane.
You want to talk to her about the weekend.
You'll phone back later.

MESSAGE 2
You want to speak to Dave.
You want to ask him to meet for a coffee at 11 o'clock tomorrow.
You want him to call you back, so you leave your phone number.

'Well, if I called the wrong number, why did you answer the phone?'

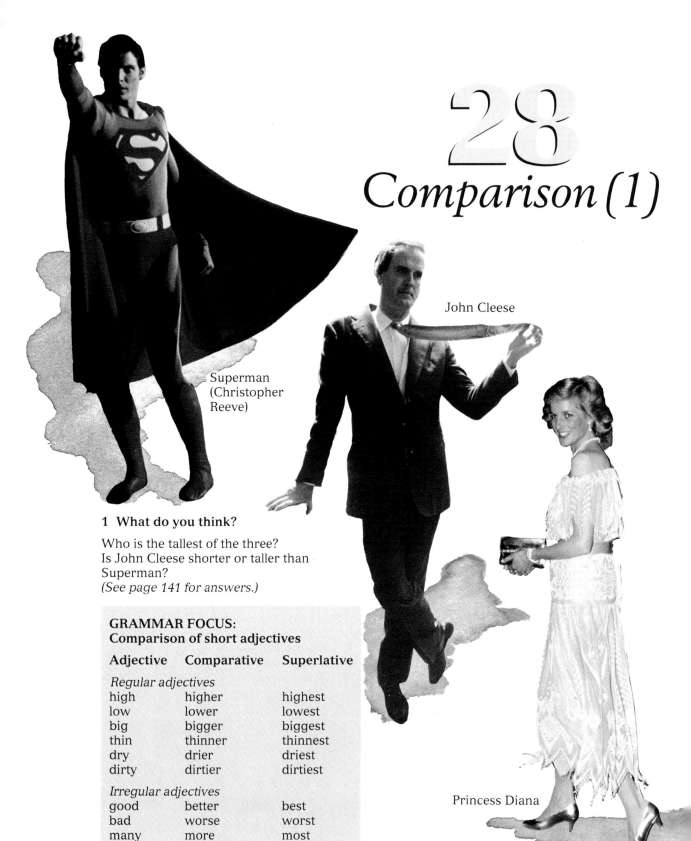

28
Comparison (1)

Superman
(Christopher
Reeve)

John Cleese

Princess Diana

1 What do you think?

Who is the tallest of the three?
Is John Cleese shorter or taller than
Superman?
(See page 141 for answers.)

GRAMMAR FOCUS:
Comparison of short adjectives

Adjective	Comparative	Superlative
Regular adjectives		
high	higher	highest
low	lower	lowest
big	bigger	biggest
thin	thinner	thinnest
dry	drier	driest
dirty	dirtier	dirtiest
Irregular adjectives		
good	better	best
bad	worse	worst
many	more	most
little	less	least

**What do you notice about the spelling
of the comparative endings of:**
big   thin   dry   dirty

2 What are the comparative and superlative forms of these adjectives?

young   small   short   fat   clean   easy
heavy   hot   cold   cheap

3 Look at the list of topics in the chart and think of people and things to compare. Use the adjectives in brackets.

Gino is taller than Juan.

STUDENTS (tall)
CITIES IN SUMMER (hot)
RIVERS (long)
CLUBS/RESTAURANTS (good)
SPORTS (easy)
CITIES IN WINTER (cold)
BUILDINGS (old)
CLOTHES SHOPS (cheap)

4 Discuss each of the categories in the chart using *who, what, which* and *where* as appropriate.

Who is the tallest student in your class?
What is the easiest sport to learn?
Where is the hottest place in summer in your country?

5 🔲 SPEECHWORK

Listen and underline the stressed syllables. Then listen and repeat.

He's taller than me.
He's thinner than her.
She's younger than you.
I'm older than him.
It's better than that.
It's cheaper than this.

6 READING

Read and find out why British people like to visit other countries for their holidays.

REASONS FOR GOING ABROAD

- The weather is better.
- The food is better – in particular, the fish is fishier and the meat is meatier.
- The people are happier and more polite.
- The wine is cheaper.
- The bars stay open later.
- The sea is warmer, bluer and cleaner.
- The night life is livelier.
- The markets are busier and noisier.
- The countryside is prettier.
- And so many ordinary things are different – breakfast, street signs, postboxes, the ringing of the telephones, matches, newspapers, bread. In fact, nothing is ordinary at all.

Do you agree with any of the statements? If so, of which places or countries do you think the statements are true?

I think the weather in Sardinia is better than the weather in the South of France.

7 In groups, discuss why you think people like to visit your country.

They think that the food is . . ./the weather is . . .

8 WRITING

Complete this advertisement for your country or a place in your country.

COME TO SUNNY . . .
where the . . . is . . . -er
where the . . . are . . . and
the . . . are . . . -er.
Relax on the . . .
Enjoy the . . .
Make all your dreams come true in . . .
The . . . place in the world for your summer holiday.
You know you deserve it!

29
Comparison (2)

1 Which is the most expensive city in the world? Which do you think is more expensive – New York or Geneva? Read and find out.

THE WORLD'S...

most expensive cities	cheapest cities
1 Tokyo (Japan)	52 Bogota (Colombia)
2 Osaka (Japan)	53 Harare (Zimbabwe)
3 Teheran (Iran)	54 Bombay (India)
4 Libreville (Gabon, West Africa)	55 Asunçion (Paraguay)
5 Brazzaville (The Congo)	56 Budapest (Hungary)
6 Douala (The Cameroon)	Mexico City (Mexico)
7 Oslo (Norway)	57 Belgrade (Yugoslavia)
8 Helsinki (Finland)	Quito (Ecuador)
9 Dakar (Senegal)	58 Buenos Aires (Argentina)
10 Geneva/Zurich (Switzerland)	59 São Paulo (Brazil)
	60 Rio de Janeiro (Brazil)
	61 Caracas (Venezuela)

These results are based on a shopping basket of food and household items, alcoholic drinks, tobacco, clothes, entertainment and transport. The survey included sixty-one major cities.

The most expensive US city is New York at 23, followed by Los Angeles at 26. In Europe, Oslo is the most expensive city at number 7. London and Paris come in at 16, Berlin at 17, and Frankfurt and Milan at 19.

GRAMMAR FOCUS: Comparison of longer adjectives

Adjective	Comparative	Superlative
expensive	more expensive	most expensive
	less expensive	least expensive

Expressions of comparison
... is more/less expensive than ...
... is the most/least expensive city in the world.

2 About you

1 Where is your capital city in the list?
2 If it isn't there, where do you think it comes?
3 How does your city compare with Oslo, New York and Rio de Janeiro?

3
Choose three towns or cities, either in your country or anywhere else in the world. Compare them using these adjectives:

beautiful interesting lively noisy polluted dangerous fashionable expensive

A: Milan is more fashionable than Bologna.
B: Yes, but Bologna is more beautiful.

4 WRITING

An English-speaking friend of yours works for a multinational company and is coming to live in your city. Your friend has a young family and wants to know if it is better to live in the centre or in the suburbs. Complete the letter.

You asked me if it is better to live in the centre or the suburbs. I think it is better to ... because ...

Japan is one of the most adaptable nations on earth. In 1945, two atomic bombs fell on Hiroshima and Nagasaki and left Japan in ruins. But today Japan has the second largest economy in the world.

Japan's list of achievements is impressive: it builds more ships and makes more cars and motorbikes than any other country; one out of every three television sets in Britain is made in Japan; it is the most famous country in the world for audio, video and photographic equipment and is a world leader in many areas of new technology. It is not surprising that the Japanese are proud of their achievements.

5 READING

Before you read

1 Name three cities in Japan.
2 What countries are its nearest neighbours?
3 What products do you associate with Japan?

Read and note three of Japan's achievements.

6 🔲 LISTENING

Before you listen

Look at the picture of the world's longest and most luxurious car. It is owned by a Japanese businessman. In groups, discuss what you think there is inside the car.

Now listen and find out.

WORKING THE WORLD

Many young people do not want to go straight to college or a job after they leave school. They want to learn about the world before they settle down. Some join international organisations to work in other countries.

ANNABEL YOUNG

Home town:	Surbiton, England
Temporary job:	teaching English in a primary school in Honduras
Accommodation:	in a room in the school
Spare time activity:	learning to scuba dive
Plan:	to travel south through Central America

Annabel says:
'I'm just beginning to settle down here in Honduras. I'm working hard but I'm having a great time. Honduras is one of the countries of Central America. People here speak mainly English and Spanish. When I leave here I'm going to visit some more countries in Central America.'

JULIEN LE GRAND

Home town:	Bordeaux, France
Temporary job:	working on a sheep farm in Queensland, Australia
Accommodation:	in a bungalow on the farm
Spare time activity:	learning to fly a light aircraft
Plan:	to explore the Great Barrier Reef

Julien says:
'Life in the Australian outback is tough. The hours are long. It's hot and there are flies everywhere. The farm is very remote. It's a bit lonely sometimes. I'm doing a lot of horse-riding and in my spare time I'm learning to fly a light aircraft. We go shopping by aeroplane because Queensland is so big. It's a hard life but it's fun!'

Temporary activities

1 READING

Before you read

At what age do most people leave school in your country?
How old are most students when they go to university or college?

Read the article and answer the questions.

1 What do many young people want to do after they leave school?
2 What is Annabel doing?
3 Where is she living?
4 What is Julien doing?
5 Why is it tough?
6 Why does he go shopping by aeroplane?

GRAMMAR FOCUS: Present continuous and present simple

Look at the sentences below and say which describes a temporary situation and which describes a permanent situation.

1 Julien is living on a farm in Australia.
2 Julien lives in Bordeaux, France.

The **present continuous** is often used to talk about temporary activities.
The **present simple** is used to talk about permanent or long-term situations.

---

2 In pairs, roleplay conversations with Annabel and Julien.

A: Where do you come from, Annabel?
B: From Surbiton in England.

3 ▣ SPEECHWORK

Which do you hear: sound 1 or 2?
1 = /ɪ/ as in live   2 = /iː/ as in leave

4 ▣ LISTENING

Listen to someone who is living and working in Britain, and complete the information in the chart.

Name: Jean Pierre

Nationality:

Temporary activities:

Permanent job:

Countries visited in his job:

5 WRITING

OXFORD STREET HOTEL
CHAMBERMAIDS
Male or female
wanted in central London hotel. Age 18 +. To serve breakfasts and clean hotel bedrooms. Live in hotel. Must speak some English. Free time (afternoon) for English language classes. Earn £70 per week! Tel 491 9987.

The girl in the photograph is a friend of yours. She gets the job in the advertisement above. Write about her in a letter. Say what she is doing in London (give details), where she is living, how much she is earning and what she is doing in her spare time.

By the way, I forgot to tell you about Carmen. Did you know she's in London? She's working as a . . .

Now write about someone you know who is living, working or studying away from home.

Fluency
UNITS 26-30

1 DIAL A CONVERSATION

In pairs, A and B choose a number on the telephone 1–9. Each of you must find the instructions for the conversation which matches that number. Do not look at your partner's instructions. Act your conversation.

8 Telephone your friend, B, who lives in another country. Give some up-to-date news about members of your family. Say where they are living and what they are doing at the moment.

2 You want to buy a cat or a dog. You telephone B to find out which he/she thinks is a better pet.

6 Telephone B. He/She isn't in. Leave a message on the answerphone about a party you are having next weekend. Give details and ask B to phone you back.

5 Find out what B is doing next Sunday.

7 You work in an office with a man called David. David isn't in the office at the moment. You think he's visiting his mother in hospital. The telephone rings. Answer the phone and take a message for him.

9 B phones you to ask for some information about your country. Try to give the correct answers!

1 You have two tickets to see the opera, *Carmen* next Thursday at La Scala, in Milan. Ask B what he/she is doing that evening (give the day and date) and if he/she would like to go with you.

3 You want to meet B one Saturday evening. Find out what B is doing on the next three Saturday evenings.

4 You want to go on a cycling holiday somewhere in your country. Try to persuade B to go with you.

STUDENT B

4 You want to go on holiday in your 'camper van'. Try to persuade A that this is the best type of holiday.

7 You are going to the cinema this evening with your friend David. You are planning to meet at 7.15 p.m. but you are going to be about ten minutes late. You telephone him at work but he isn't in. Leave a message with Student A.

1 A invites you to the opera next Thursday. You are busy that evening. Refuse politely and explain what you are doing that evening.

6 Listen to A's message on your answerphone. You phone A back but A is out. Leave your message on A's answerphone.

8 A is a friend of yours. He/She telephones you from another country. Ask A about his/her parents, brother and sister and what they are doing now.

5 You are planning to run a mini-marathon next Sunday to earn money for International Children's Day. Tell A about it and ask him/her to give you some money for each kilometre (e.g. 25p a kilometre).

9 You are writing a report. You need to know the highest mountain and the longest river in A's country. Phone A and ask him/her for the information.

3 A wants to meet you one Saturday evening. Look at your diary and tell A if you are free on the dates he/she mentions. If not, say what you are doing on those dates.

2 A phones to ask which you think is better to keep as a pet: a cat or a dog. Give your opinion.

2 NOUGHTS AND CROSSES

Play in pairs. You must try to stop your partner from completing a line of noughts or crosses horizontally (↔), vertically (↕) or diagonally (↘).

bad	small	good
dangerous	hot	expensive
dirty	polluted	cold

Follow these instructions.

1 Copy the diagram into your notebooks.
2 Decide who is going to play with a nought (0) and who is going to play with a cross (×).
3 Student A chooses a square and makes a sentence using the comparative form of the adjective, e.g. *Moscow is **colder than** Rio de Janeiro*. If the sentence is grammatically correct, A puts a × (or 0) on the square. If the sentence is wrong, A puts nothing on the square.
4 Student B now chooses another square and makes a sentence. Continue as in 3.
5 The person who first makes a line of noughts or crosses is the winner.

Check

UNITS 26-30

1 Choose the correct word to complete the telephone conversation.

Example
1 MRS GIBSON: Hello. . . . is York 88731.
      a) It (b) This c) Here

1 MRS GIBSON: Hello . . . is York 88731.
      a) It b) This c) Here

2 ADAM: . . . I speak to Laura please?
      a) Can b) Will c) Do

3 MRS GIBSON: . . . she's out at the moment.
      a) She's sorry, b) I'm sorry,
      c) So sorry,

4 ADAM: What time . . . back?
      a) is she coming b) she comes
      c) did she come

5 MRS GIBSON: I'm sorry, I . . .
      a) not know b) can't know
      c) don't know

6 ADAM: Oh, . . . a nuisance!
      a) she's b) it's c) that's

7 MRS GIBSON: . . . , please?
      a) Who speaks b) Who
      speaking c) Who's
      speaking

8 ADAM: . . . Adam. I'm a friend of hers.
      a) It's b) He's c) Here's

9 MRS GIBSON: Can I . . . a message?
      a) leave to her b) give to her
      c) give her

10 ADAM: Yes, please. Tell her . . . back later.
      a) I call b) I'll call c) I'm calling

2 Complete the sentences with the comparative form of the adjectives in brackets.

Example
1 It's (cheap) by car than by train.
1 It's cheaper by car than by train.

1 It's (cheap) by car than by train.
2 The prices are (expensive) this year than last year.
3 Many people think nurses work (hard) than doctors.
5 Which river is (long) – the Thames or the Seine?

6 Have this armchair. It's (comfortable) than that one.
7 I think the Science Museum is (interesting) than the Natural History Museum.
8 My new job is (good) than my old one.
9 We're moving to a (big) office next year.

3 Complete the sentences with the superlative form of the adjectives in brackets.

Example
1 1989 was the (hot) year on record.
1 1989 was the hottest year on record.

1 1989 was the (hot) year on record.
2 When is the (wet) month in your country?
3 New York is one of the (exciting) cities in the world!
4 The (tall) person in our family is my younger brother.
5 What's the (long) river in China?
6 The Rhine is one of the (polluted) rivers in the world.
7 The (bad) part of the journey is between Singapore and Sydney.
8 Florida has some of the (beautiful) beaches in the USA.
9 She's one of my (good) friends.

4 Complete the sentences with *a, an, the* or – (no article).

Example
1 He's working for . . . international organisation.
1 He's working for an international organisation.

1 He's working for . . . international organisation.
2 She's . . . teacher in . . . English-speaking school in Vienna.
3 Can I leave . . . message for Nina?
4 He wants to explore . . . Great Barrier Reef.
5 What's . . . weather like in Ibiza in September?
6 She wants to travel round . . . world.
7 Juan is . . . tallest student in the class.
8 She doesn't want to go straight to . . . college after she leaves . . . school.

5 Write the dates.

Example
1 6/3/91
1 6th March 1991

1 6/3/91	4 31/7/64	7 15/8/88
2 24/11/89	5 22/2/75	8 9/10/49
3 12/4/99	6 3/9/39	9 23/1/72

6 Choose the correct words to complete the letter.

April 13th

Dear Richard,

I heard from Martin that you and Elsa (1) . . . to London this summer for a holiday. Penny and I (2) . . . on holiday on August 2nd for a week. If you are in London then, (3) . . . to use our flat? It's quite (4) . . . the underground. We (5) . . . very hard at the moment so we really need a holiday! Write soon and let us know if you want the flat.

Yours,
Rob

1 a) will come   (b) are coming   c) come
2 a) are going   b) going   c) go
3 a) do you like   b) you want   c) would you like
4 a) close   b) near   c) next to
5 a) work   b) are working   c) are going to work

7 Rewrite the letter putting in the correct punctuation: full stops, capital letters and question marks.

Dear Tom,
I'm arriving . . .

dear tom
   im arriving on monday, october 4th and taking the train to leeds ill call you and arrange a time to meet how was your summer
yours, sam

CHECK YOUR PROGRESS

Add up your score. How well did you do?

Easy exercises . . .
Difficult exercises . . .
Problems . . .

LEARNING TO LEARN 6: Making mistakes

Making mistakes is a natural part of learning a new language. But it is important to learn from your mistakes. This is how you can do this:

1 If you make a mistake when you speak, always repeat the correct form.

2 If you make a mistake when you write, always rewrite the correct form.

I went to England for to learn English.   X (WRONG)

- Find your mistake. Is it a spelling, grammar or vocabulary mistake?
- Write the complete sentence again correctly, e.g.
  I went to England to learn English.
- Make a note of the sort of mistakes you make most often. When you do written homework, check these points especially.

Answer the questions.

1 What happens to Laura?
2 Who helps her?
3 Where does he take her?
4 What does he offer her?
5 How does she feel?
6 How does she get home?

In Units 31–35 you will learn how to:

– offer and order food and drink
– ask and talk about recent events
– ask and talk about experiences
– talk about illness and discomfort
– talk about things you've got to do

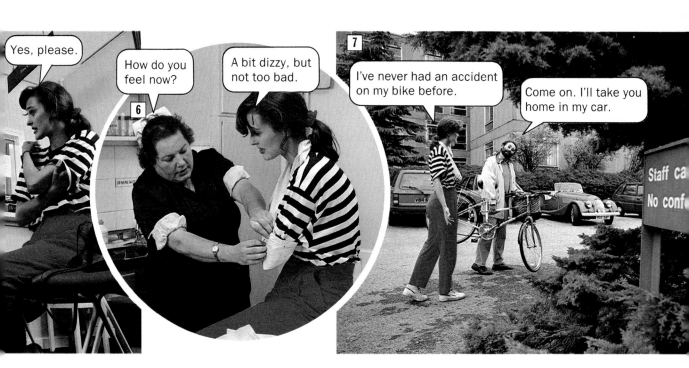

31
Eating out

1 Look at the pictures. What do you think the people are saying? Match the sentences below with each picture.

Yes. I think I'll have the chicken.
Here are your coffees.
What would you like to drink?
No, thank you. No desserts. Just coffee.
Thank you. And can we have the bill too, please?
Are you ready to order now?
Could we have a lager and a glass of white wine, please?
Would you like a dessert?

Write the completed dialogue.

2 🔲 LISTENING

Now listen to the dialogue and note three differences.

COMMUNICATION FOCUS: Offering and requesting

Would you like to order now?	I think I'll have (the) chicken.
What would you like to drink?	I'd like (an) orange juice, please.
	Can I have (some) water, please?
	Could I have (a) lager, please?
Would you like a dessert?	Yes, please./No, thank you.

---

3 🔲 SPEECHWORK

Which do you hear?

1 I or I'd   4 She'd or She
2 I or I'll   5 He's or His
3 I or I'm   6 I or I'll

Now listen and repeat the sentences.

4 In pairs, select hot or cold drinks from the automatic machine.

A: Would you like something to drink?
B: Yes, please.
A: What would you like?
B: I'd like/I think I'll have coffee, please.
A: With milk and sugar?
B: No, thanks. Black, please, and no sugar.

5 ROLEPLAY

In groups, make your own menu, or use the one below, to roleplay ordering a meal in a restaurant.

The Grapevine

STARTER
French onion soup
Orange and tomato salad
Prawn cocktail

MAIN COURSE
Fillet steak
Lamb kebab
Chicken Kiev
Mushroom risotto
All main dishes served with vegetables and a choice of rice or potatoes.

DESSERT
Fresh fruit salad
Chocolate mousse
Ice cream

Red or white wine by the glass or bottle
Mineral water
Selection of beers and lagers

Service not included.

6 READING

Before you rea

Are there any fc
   restaurants in
What sort of res
   you like?
What sort of take-away food
   do you usually eat?

Read and answer the questions.

1 Why are Thai, Korean and Japanese restaurants popular?
2 Where does the idea of take-away food come from?

ABOUT EATING OUT IN BRITAIN

British eating habits are very different now from thirty years ago. People travel more and are learning to enjoy food from many different countries. In most towns, there are Chinese and Indian restaurants but in big cities you can also eat Japanese, Thai, Korean and Malaysian food. These restaurants are often cheaper than European restaurants and many people think that the food is more interesting.

Take-away food is also very popular in Britain. Many people think that the idea of take-away meals comes from the USA, but in fact it comes from Britain. The original British take-away meal was fish and chips and there are still fish and chip shops everywhere, as well as restaurants selling fast food like pizzas and hamburgers.

32

Recent events

1 🔲 LISTENING

Before you listen

Mrs Gibson has just had some good news.
What do you think has happened?

1 She has just won a competition.
2 She has just passed an exam.
3 She has just received some money.

**Now listen and find out why Mrs Gibson is
so happy.**

**GRAMMAR FOCUS:
Present perfect tense**

Question	*Positive*
What has she/he won?	She/He has (just) won a competition.
	Negative
	She/He hasn't won a competition.
	Short answer
Has she/he won?	Yes, she/he has. No, she/he hasn't.

---

2 Use the list of verbs to say what has happened in each picture.

break	broke	broken
lose	lost	lost
drop	dropped	dropped
hurt	hurt	hurt
find	found	found
see	saw	seen

A: What has he done?
B: He's broken a cup.

1 cup	3 leg
2 magazine	4 £5

3 🔲 SPEECHWORK

**Listen and repeat these words. Notice the
/h/ sound.**

he's	his	have	has	had
here	hair	hurt		

he's had a nice time   he's hurt his leg

4 Mime something unfortunate which has just happened to you, e.g. you've just broken your watch. Other students guess what it is by asking *Yes/No* questions.

A: Have you lost something?
B: No, I haven't.
A: Have you broken something?
B: Yes, I have.

1 START HERE

2

3 You see a dolphin. Move on 1.

4

5 You drop your wallet in the sea. Move back 3.

6

12

11 You hurt your leg in the swimming pool. Move back 3.

10

9

8

7 You lose your passport. Move back 2.

13 You have coffee with a famous actor. Move on 3.

14

15 You have dinner at the captain's table. Move on 6.

16

17 You lose £100 at roulette. Move back 7.

18

24

23

22 You lose your camera. Move back 4.

21

20 You win the ship's lottery. Move on 4.

19

25 You see a beautiful beach. Miss a turn.

26

27

28 You break your sunglasses. Miss a turn.

29

30 You win a camera in a competition. Move on 3.

36 FLY HOME

35 You drop your book into the swimming pool. Move back 4.

34

33 You see land. Move on 1.

32

31

5 Caribbean cruise

This is a game for groups of two to six players. You need a counter for each person, e.g. a coin or button, and a dice for each group. Throw the dice to see who starts. If you land on an 'information' square, you must say what has just happened. You must throw the exact number to finish.

A: (*Lands on square 3*) I've just seen a dolphin. It says 'Move on 1'.

B: It's my turn now. (*Lands on square 5*) Oh no!

A: What's happened?

B: I've just dropped my wallet in the sea. It says 'Move back 3'.

102

SOME OF TODAY'S WONDERS OF THE WORLD

33
Experiences

1 Look at the photographs and identify the places.

The Sugar Loaf mountain, Rio
The Colosseum, Rome
The Great Barrier Reef, Australia
The Great Wall of China
The Floating Market, Bangkok
The Taj Mahal, India
The temples of Kyoto, Japan

2 In pairs, discuss if you have seen any of these famous places and sights.

A: I've seen the Sugar Loaf mountain in Rio.
Have you ever seen it?
B: No, I haven't. I've never been to Brazil.

GRAMMAR FOCUS: Present perfect with *ever*

The present perfect is used to ask and talk about experiences.

Question	*Short answer*
Have you ever seen a big waterfall?	Yes, I have.
Have you ever been to Africa?	No, I haven't.

	Positive and negative
How many times have you seen this film?	I've seen it three times.
	I've never seen it.
How many times have you been to Rio?	I've been twice.
	I've never been there.

Where do the words *ever* and *never* come in the sentence?

Note
He's **been** to Rio twice, not ~~He's gone to Rio twice.~~
He's been to Rio, means that he's gone and come back.
He's gone to Rio, means that he is still in Rio and has not yet come back.

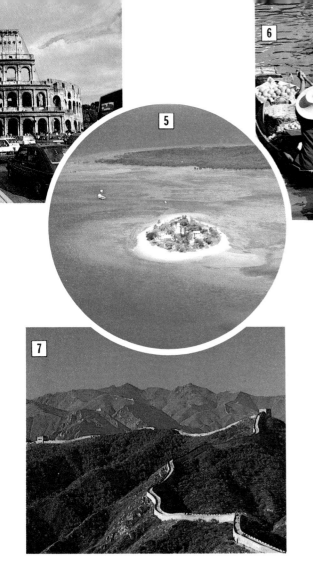

5 🔊 LISTENING

Listen to a conversation between Adam and Laura and answer the questions. Use the list of places in York to help you.

The Jorvik Centre   Howard's End
The Railway Museum   York Minster
The Castle Museum   Clifford's Tower

1 What is Laura planning to go and see?
2 Has Adam been to see it?
3 What is the only famous place he has been to in York?

6 About you

Have you seen all the famous places and sights in your town/area? If so, how many times have you seen them?

7 WRITING

Michael has just received a letter from a friend in Kenya. Copy and complete the letter using the present perfect of the verbs in brackets.

Dear Michael,

Thanks for your postcard from Spain. I'm sorry I (not write) before but I (be) very busy and very hot! Gerry's parents are here and we're doing a lot of sightseeing. They (read) a few guide books and they want to see everything. We (do) quite a lot so far. We (be) to Mombasa on the coast, we (climb) the foothills of Mount Kilimanjaro and we (fly) over the Victoria Falls in Zimbabwe. At the moment I'm writing this letter on safari in the Serengeti National Park. We (just see) some lions! By the way, (you ever sleep) under a mosquito net? It's great fun! Anyway, I must go, Gerry's dad thinks he (find) a scorpion in his sleeping bag!

Love,

Emma

3 🔊 SPEECHWORK

Underline the stressed syllables.

Have you ever seen it?   Have you ever read it?   Have you ever been there? Have you ever tried it?

Now listen and repeat the phrases.

4 Note down your answers to these questions.

Have you read any good books or seen any good films recently?
Have you been anywhere interesting or tried any unusual food or drink?
Have you done anything exciting or unusual?

Find two people in your class who have enjoyed or done the same things as you. Ask for an opinion from each person.

A: Have you ever read . . . by . . .?/seen . . .?/ been to . . .?
B: Yes, I have.
A: Did you enjoy it?
B: Yes, I did./No, I didn't. I thought it was . . .

34
Illness and discomfort

1 What do you think is the matter with the person in the photograph above?

2 What do you think is the matter with the boy in the pictures?

In which picture has he got:
– a stomachache?   – a headache?
– a cold?   – a cough?

3 💻 **LISTENING**

Listen to the advertisement. What is it for?

4 In pairs, use the Focus box to ask and say what the matter is and offer help.

COMMUNICATION FOCUS:

Asking what's wrong
What's the matter?
Are you all right?

Saying what's wrong
I don't feel very well.
I feel sick/ill/very hot/dizzy/tired.
I've got a headache/a cold.
         a sore throat/a cough.
         a temperature/a stomachache.
I've hurt my arm/leg.

Offering help
Would you like a glass of water/a tissue ?
         an aspirin/some cough medicine?
         to sit/lie down?
         to go home/go to bed?
         to take an aspirin?
         to see a doctor?

5 Use the photograph to identify the parts of the body.

head   nose   throat   eye   mouth   neck
shoulder   arm   hand   wrist   finger
thumb   elbow   leg   knee   ankle   foot
toe   back   stomach

5 ROLEPLAY

In pairs, write a dialogue for the following situation.

A telephones B to invite her/him to play squash/tennis/football. Unfortunately B doesn't feel well (temperature/sore throat) or has had an accident and has hurt something (arm/leg).

Start like this:

A: Hello. Is that . . .?
B: Yes, it is.
A: It's . . . here. Would you like to play . . .?
B: I'm afraid I can't.
A: Oh, what . . .?

Now roleplay your conversation for the rest of the group. Try not to look at your written dialogue.

7 ▣ SPEECHWORK

Underline the main stress in these words. Which syllable in each word is reduced (i.e you can't hear it)? Listen and see if you were right.

temperature   medicine   different
restaurant   dictionary   interesting

8 WRITING

Work in pairs. Write a note to your partner inviting him/her to the cinema with you tomorrow evening. Exchange notes. Reply to your partner's invitation, saying why you can't go to the cinema.

Dear . . .
Thanks for inviting me to . . . I'm afraid I can't come because . . .
Yours,

9 About you

1 When were you last ill? What was the matter?
2 What do you do when you have a cold? What medicines do you take?
3 What do you take for a headache?

10 READING

Read the instructions for a cold remedy and note the correct answers.

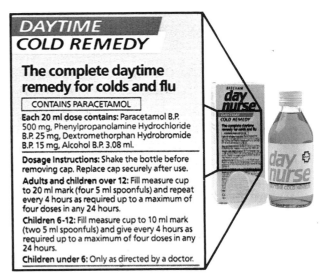

DAYTIME COLD REMEDY

The complete daytime remedy for colds and flu

CONTAINS PARACETAMOL

Each 20 ml dose contains: Paracetamol B.P. 500 mg, Phenylpropanolamine Hydrochloride B.P. 25 mg, Dextromethorphan Hydrobromide B.P. 15 mg, Alcohol B.P. 3.08 ml.

Dosage Instructions: Shake the bottle before removing cap. Replace cap securely after use.

Adults and children over 12: Fill measure cup to 20 ml mark (four 5 ml spoonfuls) and repeat every 4 hours as required up to a maximum of four doses in any 24 hours.

Children 6-12: Fill measure cup to 10 ml mark (two 5 ml spoonfuls) and give every 4 hours as required up to a maximum of four doses in any 24 hours.

Children under 6: Only as directed by a doctor.

1 As an adult, how much medicine should you take each time?
   a) Four 5 ml spoonfuls.
   b) Two 5 ml spoonfuls.
   c) One spoonful.

2 How many times can you take the medicine in 24 hours?
   a) Once.
   b) Six times.
   c) Four times.

35 Things to do

1 Match the things to do on Adam's list with the places above.

1 bank

2 Use Adam's list to say what he has got to do.

He's got to go to the bank to cash a cheque.

Things to do

1 Cash cheque
2 Buy toothpaste
3 Buy stamps
4 Collect photos
5 Buy birthday card for Mum
6 Return video
7 Buy newspaper

GRAMMAR FOCUS: *Have got to*

Positive
I've got to go to the bank.

Question	*Short answer*
Have you got to go now?	Yes, I have.
	No, I haven't.

Have got to means that it is necessary or important to do something. It is often used when making excuses, e.g. *I can't come. I've got to do some work.*

Infinitive of purpose
The infinitive with *to* is used to talk about why we want to do things.

I've got to go to the bank **to get** some Eurocheques.
She's going to Britain **to learn** English.

3 Discuss other reasons why you can go to a bank, a post office, a chemist's or a newsagent's.

A: You can go to a bank to get travellers' cheques.
B: Or to change money.

4 Make a list of five things you have got to do in the next few days at different places. Then talk about them.

A: I've got to go to the chemist's.
B: Really. Why?
A: To buy some aspirin and a new toothbrush.

5 🖭 LISTENING

Mrs Gibson wants Adam to give her some advice about her holiday. Laura telephones Adam to arrange a time to come and talk to Mrs Gibson.

Listen and find out when he can come. Copy and complete the information with a tick (✓) for *Yes* or a cross (✗) for *No*.

	Adam	Mrs G.	Reason
This evening			
Tomorrow evening			
Friday evening			

6 ROLEPLAY

STUDENT A
You work in a travel agent's office. Student B wants to fly to Madrid. The weekday morning and evening flights between London and Madrid are as follows:

SPAIN	
Departs London	**Arrives Madrid**
0830	1150
1145	1445
Departs Madrid	**Arrives London**
1705	1815
2035	2150
Check-in time is 1 hour 30 minutes before departure time.	

STUDENT B
You are in London. You go into a travel agent's to book a flight to Madrid for next Friday. You've got to be in Madrid at half past twelve in the morning and back in London at half past ten in the evening. You would also like to know what time you've got to check in at the airport in London.

A: Can I help you?
B: Yes, I'd like to book a flight to Madrid next Friday.
A: Yes, what time of day do you want to travel?

7 WRITING

Some elderly friends of your family have invited you to come to lunch next Saturday. Unfortunately it is your cousin's wedding that day. Write a letter to your friends, using the guide below.

PARAGRAPH 1
Thank your friends for the invitation. Say what for and when.
PARAGRAPH 2
Say that you can't come and explain why.
PARAGRAPH 3
Invite them to come and have tea/coffee with you sometime. Suggest when.
END YOUR LETTER
Best wishes,

Dear Mr and Mrs . . . ,
Thank you very much for inviting me to . . .

I'm afraid . . . because . . .

Fluency

UNITS 31-35

1 READING

Dave is on a trip from London to Hong Kong via Amsterdam. Read a letter from Dave to a friend about his impressions of Amsterdam and answer the following questions.

1 What is his hotel like?
2 Who did he meet on the plane?
3 What has he seen and done in Amsterdam?
4 What is the weather like?

> The Koenig Hotel,
> Amsterdam,
> Holland
>
> 30th July
>
> Dear Cathy,
>
> I'm writing in my hotel here in Amsterdam. The hotel is quite small but it's situated near the harbour and there's a wonderful view from my window.
>
> The flight was very short from London. It only took an hour. I met an interesting Dutchman on the plane. He told me a lot about the city. In fact, we're meeting this afternoon to go to an art gallery. Amsterdam is a fascinating city. There's so much to see. I've travelled along the canals, I've seen the old university and I've been to an open-air market.
>
> The weather's quite warm but a bit cloudy. Tomorrow I'm catching the plane to Hong Kong.
>
> Life is great! See you soon.
>
> Love,
>
> Dave

HONG KONG AT A GLANCE

New Territories
Kowloon

▲ Victoria Peak
Hong Kong Island

Position:	On the south-east coast of China
Population:	6,000,000
Capital:	Victoria
Currency:	Hong Kong Dollar
Languages:	Chinese (Cantonese) and English
Government:	Until 1997: British Crown Colony After 1997: part of Communist China
Climate:	Subtropical: it rains from May to September. Temperatures from 14°C in February to 30°C in July/August
Main exports:	Clothing, electronic goods, clocks and watches, toys, plastic products

2 Look at the information about Hong Kong. Think of six questions to ask someone in the class.

Example
Where is Hong Kong situated?

3 ROLEPLAY

Imagine you are going to Hong Kong. In pairs act out the conversations.

CONVERSATION 1
A
You are vegetarian. Phone the airline and tell them where you are travelling to, when, and what you would like for lunch and dinner on the flight.

B
You work for the airline. There are three types of vegetarian meal on the menu: a cheese omelette with salad, a mushroom risotto or a vegetable lasagne.

THINGS TO DO AND SEE IN
HONG KONG

- Hong Kong Island tour: Go on a half-day tour of one of the world's most famous islands. See Victoria Peak and Repulse Bay.
- Harbour cruise: Go on a two-hour cruise around the colourful busy harbour.
- Hong Kong by night: Enjoy a Chinese dinner on board the Aberdeen floating restaurant. Then enjoy the open-air night market for fabulous bargains.

CONVERSATION 2

A

During the flight you get a very bad headache. Call the air steward. Explain what is wrong and ask for some tablets for your headache.

B

You are an air steward. A passenger calls you. Ask what is wrong and offer to get the passenger some tablets and a glass of water. Give the passenger two tablets. Explain that he/she has got to take one now and another after four hours.

CONVERSATION 3

A

You think the person in the seat next to you is from Hong Kong. You start a conversation. This is your first trip to Hong Kong and you would like to know more about it. You are staying at the Peninsula Hotel on the waterfront. You would like to know what the hotel is like.

B

You are from Hong Kong. The person sitting next to you asks you where you come from. You ask the person if he/she has ever been there before. Tell him/her what Hong Kong is like. You have never been inside any of the hotels.

CONVERSATION 4

A

You have enjoyed talking to your Hong Kong friend. You would like to meet him/her again. You are busy tomorrow and the next day because you've got to visit some friends outside Hong Kong. Suggest another day and arrange when and where to meet.

B

You would like to meet your friend again. Ask if he/she would like to have a meal with you and your family. Suggest tomorrow evening. Arrange when and where to meet.

4 🔲 LISTENING

You are soon going to land in Hong Kong. Listen to the information about your arrival. Note:

- the time of arrival in Hong Kong
- the weather
- the temperature
- what you can see from the left-hand side of the plane

5 WRITING

Dave has now arrived in Hong Kong. It is his third day there. Use the letter, the information on these pages and your imagination to write a letter from Dave to Cathy.

Check

UNITS 31-35

1 Complete the conversations with the correct tense of the verbs in brackets, present perfect or past simple.

Example
CONVERSATION 1
A: (1) (ever be) . . . to Japan?
1: Have you ever been to Japan?

CONVERSATION 1
A: (1) (ever be) . . . to Japan?
B: Yes, I have.
A: When (2) (you go) . . . ?
B: I (3) (go) . . . there in 1989. What about you?
A: I (4) (be) . . . there three times. I (5) (get) . . . relatives there.

CONVERSATION 2
A: I'm reading the latest John le Carré novel. (6) (You ever read) . . . any of his books?
B: Yes, I (7) (read) . . . 'The Russia House' on holiday last summer.
A: What (8) (you think) . . . of it?
B: I (9) (think) . . . it (10) (be) . . . very good. (11) (you like) . . . it?
A: Actually, I (12) (not read) . . . that one.

CONVERSATION 3
A: What's the matter? (13) (hurt) . . . your arm?
B: Yes. Luckily, I (14) (not break) . . . it.
A: How (15) (you do) . . . it?
B: I fell down the stairs!

2 Complete the parts of the verbs.

Example
1 go   went   . . .
1 go   went   gone

1 go	went	. . .
2 fall	fell	. . .
3 lose	lost	. . .
4 drop	dropped	. . .
5 break	broke	. . .
6 see	saw	. . .
7 find	found	. . .
8 win	won	. . .
9 have	had	. . .
10 hurt	hurt	. . .
11 eat	ate	. . .
12 read	read	. . .

3 Choose the odd word out in these parts of the body.

Example
1 eyes (back) nose ears

1 eyes back nose ears
2 arm hand elbow stomach
3 wrist ankle body knee
4 thumb mouth toe finger
5 neck throat head foot

4 Complete the sentences using the following:

a   an   the   my   his   her
your   – (no article)

Example
1 I'm sorry I can't come to the theatre. I've got . . . very bad cold.
1 I'm sorry I can't come to the theatre. I've got a very bad cold.

1 I'm sorry I can't come to the theatre. I've got . . . very bad cold.
2 Why don't you go to bed if you've got . . . temperature?
3 I've hurt . . . arm.
4 Would you like . . . aspirin?
5 Have you hurt . . . ankle?
6 He's got . . . awful headache.
7 She's hurt . . . arm.
8 He's broken . . . leg.
9 What's . . . matter?
10 I've got . . . terrible toothache.

5 Choose the best reply in the right-hand column for each sentence in the left-hand column.

Example
1 Good evening, sir.   *c) Good evening.*

1 Good evening, sir.	a) Thank you.
2 Here's the menu.	b) Some potatoes and peas, please.
3 Are you ready to order?	c) Good evening.
4 Anything else?	d) Yes, we'd both like the fish.
5 And what would you like to drink?	e) A bottle of mineral water, please.

6 Choose the correct answer.

Example

1 A: Someone told me that 'Henry's' restaurant is very good.
  B: Yes, I'm having a . . . there tomorrow.
  a) food   b) dish   (c) meal

1 A: Someone told me that 'Henry's' restaurant is very good.
  B: Yes, I'm having a . . . there tomorrow.
  a) food   b) dish   c) meal
2 The . . . looks quite good. What are you going to have?
  a) programme   b) menu   c) list
3 'Lasagne' is an Italian . . .
  a) dish   b) plate   c) course
4 . . . We're ready to order now.
  a) Waiter!   b) Boy!   c) Mr!
5 Excuse me, can I have the . . ., please?
  a) bill   b) note   c) addition

7 Choose the correct sentence.

Example

1 a) I must to go the bank.
  (b) I've got to go to the bank.

1 a) I must to go the bank.
  b) I've got to go to the bank.
2 a) I've got a bad cold, I'm afraid.
  b) I get a bad cold, I'm afraid.
3 a) Here's the menu. Would you like the fish?
  b) Here's the menu. Do you like to have the fish?
4 a) I'm afraid we haven't got some fish.
  b) I'm afraid we haven't got any fish.
5 a) She not has broken her arm.
  b) She has not broken her arm.

8 Match the two halves of the sentences.

Example

1 Sally's going to the airport
g) to meet a friend from New York.

 1 Sally's going to the airport
 2 I've got to go to the library
 3 Sam's gone to the station
 4 I'm going to the newsagent's
 5 We're going to the cafeteria
 6 She's gone to the post office
 7 I've got to go to the chemist's
 8 She's gone to the medical centre
 9 We're going to Algeria
10 They went to evening classes

a) to see Youcef's family.
b) to get the train to York.
c) to learn Italian.
d) to buy some aspirin.
e) to see the doctor.
f) to buy a magazine.
g) to meet a friend from New York.
h) to post a parcel.
i) to return my books.
j) to have a cup of tea.

CHECK YOUR PROGRESS

Add up your score. How well did you do?

Easy exercises . . .
Difficult exercises . . .
Problems . . .

LEARNING TO LEARN 7: Guessing words

When you read or listen to a new text, there may be several words you don't understand. Try to guess their meaning before you look up any words in a dictionary. Start by asking yourself these questions:

1 What sort of word is it? Is it a noun, verb, adjective or adverb?
2 Can I guess the meaning from other words? e.g.
  colourful = colour + full i.e. full of colour, interesting
  colourless = colour + less i.e. without colour, not very interesting
3 Can I guess the meaning from the context? e.g.
  I'm 'broke'. I spent my last pound on my train ticket.
  broke (in this context) = without money

Guess the meaning of the words in italics.
Gordon Sumner is an *exceptionally* good-looking man. He is very rich and so he can *afford* to buy anything he wants.

Preview

📼 Listen and follow the conversations.

Grand Summer Ball

Friday June 21st
8 p.m. – 2 a.m.
at
The Assembly Rooms
YORK

Laura,
Your ticket for the ball. See you at 7.30.
David

Don't slam the door. Just shut it gently.

Answer the questions.

1 Who sends Laura her ticket?
2 What is it for?
3 What does she buy?
4 Is Adam happy? Why?/ Why not?

In Units 36-40 you will learn how to:

– go shopping for clothes
– give instructions
– talk about rules
– talk about feelings and emotions
– talk about past events in people's lives.

36
Shopping for clothes

The re... an estimated one million | saving of £200 million, he said.

Shopping round the world

"Oh – it suits you wonderfully...."

FOR MANY Americans, shopping is a profession. Americans spend hours walking round different shops and comparing prices to see if the item they want is cheaper somewhere else.

The French are very serious about shopping. They plan everything. They know exactly what they want, how much it costs and where they are going to find it.

The British are the world's worst shoppers. They never know what they want when they go shopping, particularly when they go shopping for clothes. They always ask for advice and they believe the shop assistant who says: 'It suits you perfectly, madam.' or 'Purple is just the right colour for you, sir.'

1 About you

1 Do you like shopping for clothes? Why?/Why not?
2 Do you like shopping in small boutiques or in large department stores? Why?
3 Do you use credit cards? Why?/Why not?

2 READING

Read and decide which nationality of shoppers fit these descriptions.

Which shoppers:
– never know what they want?
– know exactly what they want?
– are always looking for a bargain (something cheap)?

3 Answer the questions about the picture.

1 Where is the man?
2 What is he trying on?
3 Is he pleased?
4 Why not?

COMMUNICATION FOCUS: Shopping

Saying what you want
I'm looking for a black jacket.

Requests
Can/Could I try this jacket on?

Saying what is wrong
It's too big/small/long/short.
It doesn't suit me.
The colour's wrong.

Asking for alternatives
Have you got a size 12?
Could you give me a smaller/larger size?
Have you got this in another colour?

Making decisions
I think I'll leave it.
I'll have/take it.

4 Look at the Focus box and complete the conversation.

ASSISTANT: Can I help you?
CUSTOMER: Yes, I'm . . . for a suit.
ASSISTANT: All the suits are over there on the left.
CUSTOMER: Thanks.
(*Later*) . . . this one on?
ASSISTANT: Yes, sure. The changing rooms are over there.
CUSTOMER: Thanks.
(*Later*)
ASSISTANT: Is it any good?
CUSTOMER: No, not really, The skirt's . . . long and anyway the . . .'s wrong. . . . it in a size 10 in black?
ASSISTANT: No, I'm sorry, we haven't. That's all we've got.
CUSTOMER: O.K. Then I'll leave it.

5 ☐ Now listen and check your conversation.

6 ☐ SPEECHWORK

Which of these words has the /uː/ sound and rhymes with *suit*?

boot foot fruit put juice do ruin guide noon

Listen and see if you were right.

7 Look at the pictures and say what is wrong with the clothes.

1 The trousers are too short./They're too short.

8 Imagine you are the people trying on the clothes in Exercise 7. In pairs, practise conversations.

A: Can I try these trousers on, please?
B: Yes, of course. The changing rooms are over there.
(*Later*)
B: Are they any good?
A: No, I'm afraid they're too short. Have you got a longer pair?

9 ROLEPLAY

Collect some outdoor clothes, e.g. jackets and coats, and put them on a desk at the front of the class. Roleplay shopping situations in front of the class.

10 ☐ LISTENING

Before you listen

Look at the following words and expressions and say what you think the radio programme is going to be about.

shopaholic spend
to become addicted (to)
pay credit cards
get into debt

Listen to part of a radio programme, *Your Mind and Body,* and answer the questions.

1 What was Patti's special problem and how did it start?
2 How did she pay for her purchases?
3 What did she do with them?
4 How did she solve her problem?

37
Instructions

> Turn right slowly and stop over there.

1 Look at the picture and answer the questions.

1 Why are Michael and Adam in the car?
2 What does Michael tell Adam to do?

COMMUNICATION FOCUS: Instructions

Positive
Drive slowly.
Please drive slowly.

Negative
Don't (Do not) drive so fast.
Please don't drive so fast.

GRAMMAR FOCUS: Adverbs

Regular		Irregular	
Adjective	*Adverb*	*Adjective*	*Adverb*
slow	slowly	good	well
careful	carefully	fast	fast
gentle	gently	early	early
happy	happily	late	late
rude	rudely	hard	hard

What are the adverbs from these regular adjectives?
quick   angry   simple   easy   beautiful   firm   polite

Position of adverbs
He usually drives **slowly**.
Don't drive **so fast**!
Close the door **quietly**.
He speaks German **very well**.

Do the adverbs of manner usually come before or after the main verb? What happens when there is a noun after the verb?

---

2 Without using words, how do you give these instructions in your language? Demonstrate to the class.

I can't hear. Speak up!	Don't make so much noise.
Come here.	Go away.
Put it over there.	Stop!
Write it down.	Come on! Sing more loudly!

3 🔲 LISTENING

Listen and say which conversation is about:

1 how to make a cake.
2 how to play a video cassette.
3 how to act a scene in a play.
4 how to answer examination questions.

Listen again and note the adverbs as you hear them. Which adverb is used most often and which is not used at all?

quickly	gently
carefully	angrily
firmly	slowly
quietly	immediately

5 READING

Before you read

Have you ever been to an interview? What was it for?
What was it like? How did you feel?
What do people often do wrong in interviews?

Read about how not to behave in an interview and answer the questions.

1 What are three common mistakes that people make?
2 Which do you think is the funniest job interview story?

Making the wrong impression

JOB INTERVIEWS are never easy but some people make the most obvious mistakes. Some arrive late. Others don't prepare what they are going to say. And many don't even show any interest in the job.

There are lots of funny stories about job interviews. According to one company, one person went into the interview wearing motorcycle clothes – including a crash helmet! Another listened to a personal stereo the whole time. A third suggested an arm-wrestling competition with the interviewer, while another just fell asleep – and snored!

4 Write an instruction and give it to someone in the class. The person must carry out the instruction. The rest of the class must say what the person is doing and how he/she is doing it.

Write your name quickly.
Drink a glass of water . . .
Draw a house . . .

6 WRITING

Complete the instructions for going to an interview in Britain. Use the correct adjectives and adverbs.

clearly   punctually   confident   smartly   nervous
carefully   comfortably   early   firmly   fast   briefly

MAKING THE RIGHT IMPRESSION

1 Dress . . . but . . . If you're a woman, don't wear too much make-up or jewellery.
2 Check the time of the interview and arrive . . .
Remember, it's better to be . . . than late.
3 When you are introduced, shake hands . . .
4 Look cheerful and . . . – even if you aren't feeling it!
5 Don't smoke.
6 Answer questions . . . but honestly.
7 Speak . . . and try not to speak too . . ., even if you are . . .
8 Listen . . . and with interest when the interviewer talks about the job.

Compare your sentences with your partner.

Do you disagree with any of these instructions?
Is it the same in your country? If not, how is it different?

1

NO SWIMMING

8

2

STOP

7
NO SMOKING

6

PLEASE

NO DOGS

NO SMOKING

NO ICES

FLASH

NO FLASH

THANK YOU

38
Rules

1 Say where you might find each notice.

1 No entry = on a road/in a street

– in a library	– in a street
– on a road	– in the country
– on an aeroplane	– in a park
– by a lake or river	– in a museum

COMMUNICATION FOCUS: Rules

Giving rules
You must fasten your seatbelts.
You can't/mustn't smoke in here.

Giving permission
You can smoke in here if you want to.

Notice the spelling and pronunciation of *mustn't* /mʌsnt/.

---

2 Say what the notices mean, using *must, mustn't* or *can*.

1 You mustn't go down that road.

3 About you

Where in your city:
– can you fish?
– can you swim in the open-air?
– can you ride a bicycle?

5

NO FISHING

3

NO PARKING PLEASE
ACCESS FOR DISABLED

FASTEN

SEAT BELT

4

PLEASE KEEP OFF THE GRASS

9

10

11

Caravan & Camping Park ➡

4 You work at a gym club. In pairs, use the cues below to make rules for the gym, sauna, and car park, using *must always* and *mustn't*.

IN THE GYM
You must always wear sports shoes and sports clothes.
You mustn't smoke.

IN THE GYM:
wear sports shoes and sports clothes
smoke
use the equipment without a teacher
use training bicycles for more than twenty
*   minutes*
clean the equipment after using it

IN THE SAUNA:
wear a swimming costume
remove any jewellery
read newspapers
use the sauna after 8 p.m.

IN THE CAR PARK:
lock your car
make any noise after 9.30 p.m.
leave your car overnight
play your car radio loudly

5 ▣ LISTENING

Listen to a young American talking about some of the rules for people who work in Disneyworld. Look at the list below and note the things which the employees can do, and the things which they mustn't do.

Moustaches   Perfume and aftershave
Beards   Smoking
Make-up   Hats

Please don't throw your cigarette ends on the floor — the cockroaches are getting cancer

6 READING

Before you read

Do you smoke? Have your ever smoked?
In which public places in your country (e.g. banks, post offices, cinemas, trains) can you smoke?
Where can't/mustn't you smoke?
What percentage of men and women smoke in your country? Is it the same?

Read the text about smoking in Britain and answer the questions.

1 Is cigarette advertising allowed on TV in Britain?
2 In which public places in Britain mustn't you smoke now?
3 Which country has the highest percentage of men who smoke?
4 Which country has the lowest percentage of women who smoke?

ABOUT SMOKING IN BRITAIN

Not long ago, the British were a nation of heavy smokers. In 1976, forty-six per cent of men smoked. Since then nine million people have stopped smoking and today only thirty-three per cent of men smoke.

Many health organisations in Britain think that this figure is still too high and they are still trying to stop more people smoking. Cigarette advertising is forbidden on television and radio; all cigarette packets and advertisements in magazines and newspapers have a government health warning: SMOKING CAN SERIOUSLY DAMAGE YOUR HEALTH; there are 'No Smoking' signs on underground trains, on buses, in cinemas, in theatres and in many banks and post offices. Some restaurants even have no-smoking areas.

Figures below show how Britain compares with other countries of the world.

Country	Percentage of men who smoke	Percentage of women who smoke
Papua New Guinea	80%	not known
China	65%	7%
Japan	61%	15%
Greece	55%	8%
France	40%	29%
Britain	35%	32%
Norway	34%	31%
USA	32%	27%

39
Feelings and emotions

1 ▣ LISTENING

Look at the pictures and listen to three short pieces of music. Choose a piece of music for each picture.

2 Do you know any of the pieces of music? How do you feel when you listen to them?

sad happy angry frightened excited
bored depressed nervous

1 When I listen to the first piece of music, I feel . . .

3 What colours do you think of when you hear the words in Exercise 2?

1 When I hear the word 'sad', I think of the colour 'blue'.

Compare your answers.

4 Use the adjectives in Exercise 2 to talk about how you feel about certain things.

A: How do you feel when you wake up on a rainy day?
B: When I wake up on a rainy day, I feel depressed.
A: Yes, I often feel depressed, too./Oh, I don't.

⁇ How do you feel when you:

1 wake up on a rainy day?
2 walk along a dark street at night?
3 find a public telephone that doesn't work?
4 go to the dentist?
5 think about your next holiday?
6 lose something valuable?
7 say goodbye to someone you love?
8 take off in an aeroplane?

121

5 READING

Before you read

Look at the scene in the photographs.

What is happening?
Where?
When do you think it happened?

Read the text and answer the questions.

1 How did the little girl feel on the train?
2 How did her mother and father feel?
3 What do you think the girl felt when she arrived at her new home? Do you think she felt homesick? excited? lonely?

6 About you

1 Do you cry when you say goodbye to people?
2 Have you (or anyone in your family) ever left home for a long time?
3 What was the reason?
4 How did you feel when you said goodbye?
5 Have you ever felt homesick?

THE DAY THE CHILDREN SAID GOODBYE

Early in September 1939, in many cities of Europe, thousands of children left their homes. Some went to live in the country, others went to live in other countries and did not see their parents again for several years. It was the beginning of the Second World War.

'I was five years old. I went to the railway station with my mum. (My dad was too upset to come and say goodbye.) I got on the train with all the other children. I had a little suitcase in one hand and my doll in the other.

I looked out of the window at Mum and cried as she stood there waving. "You're going to sleep in a nice bed tonight," she called out to me. But I didn't want to go. I wanted to stay with her. Mum started to sniff. I didn't know what to do. I looked down at my doll because I didn't want to look at Mum. I didn't want her to start crying. Mum never cried.

I looked up again to wave but the train started to move. All I could see was Mum's old blue coat moving away. Then she was gone.'

FROM RAGU TO RICHES

This is a story about two cities, one woman and tomato sauce. The story began nearly one hundred years ago in the kitchen of a small house in the ancient city of Melfi in southern Italy. It ended with one of the USA's best-selling sauces.

In July 1892, a baby girl was born in Melfi. She was called Assunta Gala. Her father, Michelangelo, and his wife Amelia had ten children altogether. Four of them died.

In those days life in southern Italy was very hard. One way of escape was a ticket to the USA. The whole family emigrated and Assunta arrived in New York on 15th May, 1914. They went straight to 'Little Italy' in New York State and settled in the city of Rochester. Assunta had no skills except cooking and she worked in her brother's restaurant for several years. In 1927 she married Giovanni Cantisano and started a family.

Immigrants leaving a barge at Ellis Island, USA.

Italians still prefer to make their own sauces.

To earn a little extra money, Assunta began to make spaghetti sauce. She used her mother's old recipe, made the sauce in her kitchen and sold it locally. Soon everyone wanted the sauce and the Cantisanos moved the 'kitchen' to a factory. They put the sauce into cans, called it 'Ragu' and sold it throughout the north-eastern states.

In 1969, an American food company bought the 'golden recipe' for over forty million dollars! Assunta began her life in poverty and died a million-airess. Her sauce was the best-selling spaghetti sauce in the whole of the USA.

Glossary

From rags to riches A rag is an old cloth. The original expression means 'from being very poor to being very rich'.

Ragu In this case is a brand name for a range of different pasta sauces.

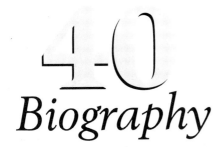

Biography

1 READING

Before you read

Look at these words and phrases. What do you think the article is going to be about?

poor Italian family   spaghetti sauce
the USA   factory   make money

Read the article and see if you were right.

2 Write ten questions to ask your partner about the story. Start your questions with *When, Where, Who, What* **and** *Why.*

1 When was Assunta born?
2 Where was she born?

3 Close your books. In groups, retell the story. Make one sentence each.

> **GRAMMAR FOCUS: Past simple with** *ago* **and** *for*
>
> The story began nearly 100 years **ago**.
> Assunta worked in her brother's
>   restaurant **for** several years.
>
> *Ago* is used to say when things happened in the past, e.g. *three days ago.*
> *For* is used to talk about length of time, e.g. *He worked there for three months.*

4 Use one of the time expressions to say when the events below happened.

about/over . . . years ago   a few years ago

A: When was the French Revolution?
B: It was over two hundred years ago.

1 The French Revolution
2 The Mexican earthquake
3 The first Moon walk
4 The Russian Revolution
5 World War II

5 Find out about some events in your partner's past life. Ask questions like:

When/Where/born?
When/Where/first start school?

6 Tell the group some facts about your partner using *in, for* **and** *ago.*

Helena was born in . . .
She first started school . . . ago.
She stayed at that school for . . . years.
After leaving school she went to university.

7 🔲 LISTENING

Before you listen

Find out the meanings of these words:

bulletin   challenging   to keep calm

Listen to an interview with TV newscaster Lisa Aziz (Unit 22) and complete the information below.

PART 1: Lisa's morning routine.

3.30   . . .
4.00   Car picks her up
. . .   Arrives in building
4.20   . . .
5.00   . . . and hair
. . .   Rehearsal
6.00   Programme starts
9.00   . . .
9.25   . . .

PART 2: Lisa's biographical details.

Name: . . .
Date of birth: 1963
Place/Country of birth: . . .
Mother's nationality: . . .
Father's nationality: . . .
Education after school (1980–83): . . .
First job (1983–4):   . . .
Present job (from Feb 1989):   . . .

8 WRITING

Use your notes to write about Lisa.

PARAGRAPH 1
Name, age and occupation
Family background
PARAGRAPH 2
Education and early career
Opinion of present job

Think of a well-known person from your country and write a similar composition.

Finale

125

Answer the questions.

1 Why is Adam angry and upset?
2 Where is Laura?
3 What does he discover about David?
4 Why did Laura go to the ball with David?
5 What is happening next week?

Signs in image:
5 to 11
Way out
Unisex toilet
Gentlemen

For Passengers' Use Only
Not To Be Removed

1 Look at the pictures. What is happening? What are they saying?

2 📼 Look at the picture on the right and listen to the conversation.

LAURA: Goodbye and thanks for everything!

MRS GIBSON: It was a pleasure. We enjoyed having you.

LAURA: I'll send you a postcard from Paris.

MR GIBSON: O.K. Bye bye! Take care!

MRS GIBSON: Have a nice time in Paris!

Now read the dialogue in threes.

3 ROLEPLAY

In pairs, prepare and practise conversations for the following situations.

SITUATION 1
You have just had dinner with your partner. Say goodbye and thank him/her for a wonderful evening. Say when you'll phone him/her.

SITUATION 2
You have stayed with your partner for a week. Say goodbye and thank him/her for everything. Say you'll send a postcard.

Example
SITUATION 1
A: Goodbye and thanks . . .
B: That's O.K. I enjoyed . . .
A: I'll . . .

Now act out your conversations.

4 🖭 LISTENING

Complete the conversation.

ADAM: . . . miss you, Laura. Can't you . . . ? Just a few more . . . ?
LAURA: I can't Adam. I've . . . go to Paris, remember? Anyway, you've got your job.
ADAM: I think I'm . . . the travel agent's.
LAURA: What . . . ?
ADAM: See the world. . . . abroad for a bit.
LAURA: . . . to?
ADAM: I don't know. Eastern Europe. Maybe Poland or Czechoslavakia.
LAURA: Or . . . California?
ADAM: Maybe.
LAURA: Please do. I'd really . . . that.
ADAM: . . . sure?
LAURA: Sure.
ADAM: The train's . . . . Phone me when you . . . to Paris.
LAURA: O.K. . . . , Adam. . . . for everything.
ADAM: Take care!

Now listen and check your conversation.

6 In pairs, make up your own farewell conversation. Act it out in front of the class.

COMMUNICATION FOCUS

Thanking
Thanks for everything.
Thanks for a wonderful day/evening/time.

Accepting thanks
It was a pleasure.
That's O.K. (informal)
I/We enjoyed it too.
I/We enjoyed having you/meeting you.

Saying goodbye
Goodbye./Bye!
I'll send you a postcard!
I'll phone you on Monday.
Have a nice holiday/time!

Check

UNITS 36–40

1 Choose the correct word on the right to complete the sentences.

Example
1 You speak English very . . .   good/well
1 You speak English very well.

1 You speak English very . . .   good/well
2 His French is very . . .   good/well
3 She waited . . . outside the room.   nervous/nervously
4 Don't speak too . . .   quiet/quietly
5 Be . . .! Someone is coming!   quiet/quietly
6 Do this exercise as . . . as possible. quick/quickly
7 Please drive . . . The roads are wet. careful/carefully
8 I must try and work . . . this term. hard/hardly
9 I'm going to get up . . . tomorrow. late/lately
10 Are you sitting . . .?   comfortable/
                                       comfortably

2 Choose the correct verb in these exchanges.

Example
1 I can't go to the disco tonight, I'm afraid. I . . . get up early tomorrow.
   a) mustn't   (b) 've got to   c) will

1 I can't go to the disco tonight, I'm afraid. I . . . get up early tomorrow.
   a) mustn't   b) 've got to   c) will

2 You . . . wear shoes in the gym.
   a) don't   b) haven't got to   c) mustn't

3 . . . go through that door. It says 'No entry'.
   a) Don't   b) Not   c) You mustn't to

4 It was a lovely party. We . . . write and thank them.
   a) got to   b) do   c) must

5 You're driving at 120 kph. You really . . . drive so fast.
   a) don't   b) didn't   c) mustn't

3 Choose the correct answer to complete the conversation.

Example
A: Can I help you?
B: Yes, I (1) look/(m looking) for a jacket.

A: Can I help you?
B: Yes, I (1) look/'m looking for a jacket.
A: What colour would you like?
B: A black or a brown (2) one/ones, maybe.
A: These are our latest jackets. What size (3) are you/have you?
B: Size 12.
A: What about this one?
B: Can I (4) try it on/wear it?
A: Yes, of course. There's a mirror over there.
(Later)
B: No, the colour (5) not suit/ doesn't suit me.
   (6) Have you got it/Is it in black?
A: Yes, but only in size 10.
B: That's a pity. Size 10 is (7) so small/too small. Have you got (8) a more large size/a larger size in other colours?
A: Yes, (9) here's/it's here a size 12 in pink.
B: Pink? Mm. No.
   I think (10) I leave/I'll leave it, thank you.

4 Write the stressed syllable in capital letters.

Example

1 MONey

1 money	6 telephone
2 address	7 beautiful
3 interesting	8 Chinese
4 hotel	9 interview
5 Japan	10 comfortable

5 Choose the correct short answers.

Example

1 Do you like Mozart?   *b) Yes, I do.*

1 Do you like Mozart?	a) Yes, I like. b) Yes, I do.
2 Would you like a sandwich?	a) Yes, I'd like. b) Yes, I'd love one.
3 Have you got any brothers?	a) No, not. b) No, I haven't.
4 Did she go to the cinema?	a) Yes, she did. b) Yes, she went.
5 Has he got a car?	a) No, he hasn't. b) No, he doesn't.
6 Are you going to bed now?	a) Yes, I am. b) Yes, I go.
7 Have you hurt your arm?	a) Yes, I have b) Yes, I did.
8 Is there a bus to York?	a) No, it isn't. b) No, there isn't.
9 Can you speak Arabic?	a) Yes, I can speak. b) Yes, I can.
10 Were her grandparents Irish?	a) Yes, they were. b) Yes, they are.

6 Complete the text with the correct form of the verbs in brackets.

Louise Walters (1) (be) *is* a medical student. She (2) (study) . . . to become a doctor. She (3) (leave) . . . university a year ago and (4) (go) . . . to Guy's Hospital in London (5) (study) . . . for three years. At the moment she (6) (work) . . . very hard but she (7) (have) . . . a good time. 'I enjoy the work because I like (8) (look after) . . . people,' she says.

Next year she (9) (have got to) . . . spend three months in another country. She (10) (go) . . . to Papua New Guinea (11) (do) . . . some research there. 'I (12) (only be) . . . to Europe before,' says Louise, 'so it (13) (be) . . . very exciting!'

Last year Louise (14) (live) . . . in a nurses' hostel but now she (15) (share) . . . a small flat with two friends. She (16) (got) . . . a boyfriend but she (17) (not want) . . . to settle down yet. 'I (18) (miss) . . . him but I really (19) (want) . . . to travel as much as possible before I become a doctor and I (20) (look forward) . . . to my time abroad very much.'

CHECK YOUR PROGRESS

Add up your score. How well did you do?

Easy exercises . . .
Difficult exercises . . .
Problems . . .

LEARNING TO LEARN 8: Learning outside the classroom

Learning English should not stop at the end of your English lesson. There are several ways to improve your English:

1 Read an English magazine or newspaper, or a simple book.
2 Listen to the BBC World Service on the radio.
3 If possible, watch English or American films with subtitles (not 'dubbed' into your language).
4 Make friends with some English-speaking people.
5 Notice how English-speaking people say things. Always carry a notebook so you can write down any interesting words and expressions.
6 Note down any questions in your notebook that you want to ask the teacher, e.g.
   • Can you say *I want that you come?* (No)
   • How do I say *Skål!* in English? (Cheers!)
   • My friend said *See you Tuesday* not *See you on Tuesday*. Is this all right? (Yes, but only in spoken English.)

Vocabulary and expressions

a little
at all
fluently
quite well
very well

What's the
matter?

ancestor
answer
family
photograph
record

Family members
(See also Unit 1)
aunt
baby
child(ren)
cousin
daughter
grandfather
grandmother
grandparents
husband
nephew
niece
son
uncle
wife

alive
big
dead
only (an . . . child)
small

have got

any
together

How many?

airport
bus driver
centre
check-in
country (opp.
town)
farm
government
hostel
house
job
musician
operator
teacher

different
grown up

look after
study

alone
at home
there

What about . . .?

album
building
card (playing)
cinema
comedy
doctor
film
horror
music
penfriend
photography
pyramid
restaurant
science fiction
war

classical
modern
romantic

agree
choose
clean
cycle
eat
enjoy
garden (v)
hate
jog
keep fit
shop
tell
travel
walk
wash up

too (+ adj)

art gallery
beach
cathedral
church
harbour
museum
nightlife
ocean
place
river
sea
shop
tourist
university
zoo

Points of the
compass
north
south
east
west

beautiful
best
boring
famous
historical
industrial
interesting
old
new

know (city/person)
like (What's it like?)

exactly
far
just

cigarette
clothes
sweets

sell

library
minute
room
weekday
window

get up
go to bed
open
stay
take (time)

only

century
clock
concert
flight
fortnight
half
hour
midday
midnight
noon
o'clock
party
quarter
second
time
timetable

arrive
close
finish
start
want

except
few
until

What time?

bed
breakfast
cafeteria
church
disco
hospital
lunch
nurse
shower
television

go home
have lunch
watch

Adverbs of
frequency
always
usually
often
sometimes
never

after (that)
asleep
before
both
every (day)
typical
How often?

accountant
bicycle
boat
bus
car
engineer
journey
kilometre
life
mile
office
plane
railway
secretary (WB)
solicitor
station
taxi
traffic
train
underground
village
work

catch
collect
deliver
depend
get home
get to work
smile
walk

Why?

away
because
by
long (time)
more

armchair
back (= rear)
bath
bathroom
bedroom
bookcase
carpet
ceiling
central heating
cooker
cupboard
curtain
dining room

door
downstairs
dressing table
floor
freezer
fridge
front
furniture
garage
garden
hall
kitchen
mansion
mirror
patio
population
roof
sink
sitting room
sofa
stairs
swimming pool
upstairs
wall
wardrobe
washbasin

own (adj)
rich

altogether

bar
cat
dog
flower
hat
holiday
postcard
radio
suntan
waiter

great
wonderful

die
drink
hope
learn
lie (down)
listen to
make
run
send
sit
stand
wear
write

all right
love (from)
maybe

early

Preview 16–20
carton
corner
juice
post office
rain
weather

thirsty

Unit 16
bottle
box
camera
can
chemist
chips
chocolate
crisps
glass
hotel
jeans
lemonade
litre
loaf
magazine
mineral water
newsagent
packet
pence
petrol
pound (money)
roll
sandwich
tissues
toothpaste
T-shirt
tube
water

cheap
cold
expensive

cost

How much?
Which?

anything else?
certainly
Could I have . . .?

Unit 17
Food and drink
bacon
banana
biscuit
bread
butter
cereal
cheese
chicken
coffee
dessert
egg
fish
hamburger
honey
marmalade
meat
milk

oil
pepper
pork
potato
salt
sausage
soup
sugar
tea
toast
vegetable
vinegar
yoghurt

cup
dessert
dish
meal
note (money)

different
lazy
main
sour
sweet

buy
disappear
get (= buy)
need
prefer

some
yourself

Unit 18
artist
bookshop
bus station
car park
clerk
death
guide book
parcel
pub
taxi rank
theatre
traveller's cheque
ruin
visitor
waterfall
writer

change (money)

across
behind
between
in front of
inside
left (on the left)
next to
opposite
outside
over
right (on the right)
under

Excuse me.
unfortunately

Unit 19
Weather words
temperature
cloud(y)
cool
dry
fog(gy)
rain(y)
snow (v)
sun(ny)
warm
wet
wind(y)

Seasons
spring
summer
autumn
winter

Months of the year
January (etc)

carnival
leaf

change (v) (of
  weather)

once
When?

Unit 20
course (of study)
dinner
mountain
ship

awful
marvellous

relax
spend (time)
sunbathe
talk

last (week)

Preview 21–25
hair
phone call
skirt

busy
dark
sorry

look at
return (a call)

all
really (= very)

Unit 21
alarm clock
atlas
bible
bracelet
electric drill
parking ticket
pet
razor
ring (jewellery)
sewing machine
stereo system

strap
watch

angry
valuable

belong to
find
lose

Unit 22
*Clothes and
  accessories*
anorak
blazer
blouse
boots
cardigan
coat
dress
jacket
jeans
jewellery
scarf
shirt
shoes
shorts
skirt
swimsuit
tie
tights
trainers
trousers
vest

allergic
best-dressed
casual
checked
dark
flowery
light
patterned
plain
smart
spotted
striped

try (= attempt)

person
a lot of
so (= therefore)

Unit 23
folk song
party
passer-by
policeman
poster
slide
trip

important
late
next (week)
too much

bring
show
smoke
take

Unit 24
beard
dad
eye
glasses
moustache

blonde
curly
fair
fat
friendly
good-looking
handsome
long (hair)
medium height
pretty
short
slim
straight
tall
thin
wavy

bump
dry
catch
cough
cross
fall
lift
look like
throw

nothing
own (on my . . .)
plenty
up
while

Unit 25
actor
bunch (of flowers)
compartment
conductor
story
stranger
suitcase

amusing
hungry
silver
strange
tired
wrong

bang (v)
crash (v)
get undressed
happen
laugh
lock
make a journey
say
shout
sleep
stop
turn
unlock
wait
wake
wash

into

Language review

PERSONAL PRONOUNS AND ADJECTIVES

Subject pronouns (Units 1, 3)

I
you
he/she/it
we
you
they

Object pronouns (Unit 9)

me
you
him/her/it
us
you
them

The 2nd person *you* is the same in the singular and plural. The 2nd person subject and object form are also the same.

Possessive adjectives (Units 1, 21)

my
your
his/her/its
our
your
their

Possessive pronouns (Unit 21)

mine
yours
his/hers
ours
yours
theirs

1 No apostrophes are used here; *its* should not be confused with *it's*, which means *it is*.
2 The possessive adjectives refer to the gender of the possessor, e.g. *This is his mother and this is his father.*

THE ARTICLE (Unit 4)

Indefinite

Singular
a letter
an orange
an address book

Definite

Singular
the letter
the orange
the umbrella

Plural
the letters
the oranges
the umbrellas

The indefinite article *a* is used before words beginning with a consonant. The indefinite article *an* is used before words beginning with a vowel. *The* is the same before consonants and vowels, and for singular and plural, e.g. *the umbrella, the boy, the chairs.*

NOUNS: SINGULAR AND PLURAL (Units 1–10)

Singular	Regular plural (s, es, ies)	Singular	Irregular plural
girl	girls	woman	women
boy	boys	man	men
house	houses	child	children
bus	buses	wife	wives
tomato	tomatoes		
country	countries		

Rules for regular plurals:
1 Most nouns add *s* to the singular form.
2 Nouns ending in *s, ch, x, sh* or *o* add *-es* to the singular form. However, foreign words ending in *o* add only an *s* to form the plural, e.g. *photo/photos, piano/pianos.*
3 Nouns ending in vowel + *y* simply add an *s*, e.g. *boy/boys.*
4 Nouns ending in consonant + *y* change to consonant + *ies*, e.g. *country/countries.*

NOUNS: COUNTABLE AND UNCOUNTABLE (Unit 17)

Countable		Uncountable
Singular	*Plural*	
a mug	some mugs	some milk
a glass	some glasses	some bread
a baby	some babies	some sugar

Uncountable nouns take a singular verb, e.g. *The bread **is** on the table.*

DEMONSTRATIVE ADJECTIVES AND PRONOUNS
(Units 1–10)

Demonstrative adjectives		Demonstrative pronouns
Singular	*Plural*	*Singular and plural*
this letter	these letters	This is a letter.
this orange	these oranges	These are letters.
that letter	those letters	That is a letter.
that orange	those oranges	Those are letters.

1 *This, that, these* and *those* agree with their nouns in number. No other adjective does this.
2 *This* and *these* usually refer to objects close to the speakers. *That* and *those* often refer to objects at some distance from the speaker.

REGULAR COMPARISON OF ADJECTIVES (Units 28, 29)

Adjective	Comparative	Superlative
high	higher	highest
expensive	more expensive	most expensive

1 Adjectives of one syllable and most adjectives of two syllables form the comparative and superlative by adding -er or -est to the adjective.
2 Adjectives of more than two syllables form the comparative and superlative by putting the words *more* or *most* before the adjective.
3 Spelling changes when adding -er or -est: If the adjective ends in a vowel + consonant, the final consonant doubles, e.g. *big – bigger.* If the adjective ends in a consonant + *y*, the *y* changes to *i*, e.g. *dirty – dirtier.*

IRREGULAR COMPARISON OF ADJECTIVES (Unit 28)

Adjective	Comparative	Superlative
good	better	best
bad	worse	worst
many	more	most
little	less	least

SPOKEN (INFORMAL) SHORT FORMS

With pronouns		With verbs + *not*	
I'm	(I am)	I'm not	(am not)
She's	(She is)	You're not	(are not)
We're	(We are)	It isn't	(is not)
I've got	(I have)	He wasn't	(was not)
She's got	(She has)	They weren't	(were not)
I'd	(I would)	I don't	(do not)
I'll	(I will)	He doesn't	(does not)
		She didn't	(did not)
		You haven't	(have not)
		She hasn't	(has not)

Short forms are used in speech and in informal written English. The apostrophe can replace one or more letters, e.g. *What's* = *What is, I'd = I would.*

He can't	(cannot)
She couldn't	(could not)
She mustn't	(must not)

VERB *TO BE* PRESENT SIMPLE (Units 1, 2, 3)

Positive statements

I	am	('m)
You	are	('re)
He	is	('s)
She	is	('s)
It	is	('s)
We	are	('re)
They	are	('re)

Negative statements

I	'm not	
You	aren't	(you're not)
He	isn't	(he's not)
She	isn't	(she's not)
It	isn't	(it's not)
We	aren't	(we're not)
They	aren't	(they're not)

1 You can't say ~~I amn't~~.
2 The 2nd person singular and plural *you* always takes a plural verb, e.g. *you are.*
3 With Yes/No questions, it is common to use a short form answer rather than just *Yes* or *No,* e.g. *Yes, I am.*

Questions

Am	I	English?
Are	you / we / they	
Is	he / she / it	

Short answers Positive

Yes,	you	are.
	I	am.
	we / they	are.
	he / she / it	is.

Short answers Negative

No,	you	aren't.
	I	'm not.
	we / they	aren't.
	he / she / it	isn't.

VERB *TO BE* PAST SIMPLE (Units 7, 19)

Positive statements

I / He / She	was	at work.
You / We / They	were	

Negative statements

I / He / She	wasn't	at work.
You / We / They	weren't	

Questions

Were	you / we / they	at work?
Was	he / she	

Short answers Positive

Yes,	I	was.
	we / they	were.
	he / she	was.

Short answers Negative

No,	I	wasn't.
	we / they	weren't.
	he / she	wasn't.

VERB *HAVE GOT* (Units 7, 24)

Positive statements

I've / You've / We've / They've / He's / She's	got two children.

Negative statements

I / You / We / They	haven't got any children.
He / She	hasn't got any children.

Question			Short answers Positive			Short answers Negative		
Have	you we they	got a sister?	Yes,	I we they	have.	No,	I we they	haven't.
Has	he she			he she	has.		he she	hasn't.

Have got is used in informal spoken English to talk about possession. It means the same as the verb *have*, e.g. *I've got a brother = I have a brother.*

MODAL VERB *CAN*

Positive statements	Negative statements
I can swim.	I can't swim.

Question	Short answer Positive	Short answer Negative
Can you swim?	Yes, I can.	No, I can't.

1 *Can* is the same with all subject pronouns, e.g. *I/you/she/he/it/we/they can.*
2 In this book, *can* is used to express:
   - ability — *I can speak English.* (Unit 6)
   - requests — *Can I have a T-shirt, please?* (Units 16, 27, 31, 36)
   - permission/prohibition — *You can/can't smoke in here.* (Unit 38)

MODAL VERB *HAVE GOT TO* (Unit 35)

Positive	Negative
I've got to go.	I haven't got to go.

Question	Short answer Positive	Short answer Negative
Have you got to go?	Yes, I have.	No, I haven't.

1 *Have got to* is often used to express non-habitual obligations, e.g. *I've got to go now, I'm late.*
2 The negative form means that there is **no** obligation to do something.

MODAL VERB *MUST* (Unit 38)

Positive	Negative
You must wear sports shoes.	You mustn't wear heavy shoes.

Question	Short answer Positive	Short answer Negative
Must I wear sports shoes?	Yes, you must.	No, you needn't.*

1 *Must* is the same with all subject pronouns.
2 *The negative form of *must* expresses prohibition, e.g. *Can I smoke in here? No, I am afraid you can't/mustn't.* To express no obligation we use *needn't* or *haven't got to* (see above).

MODAL VERB *WILL* (Units 27, 31, 36)

In this book, *will* (*'ll*) is used only in its positive form to express decisions, e.g. *I'll call back later, I'll have the chicken.*

Language review

MODAL VERB *WOULD*

Positive
I'd (would) like a cup of tea.

Question
Would you like a cup of tea?

Negative
I wouldn't like to go there.

1 *Would* is the same with all subject pronouns.
2 In this book, *would* is used to express:
   requests   *I'd like a box of tissues.*   (Units 16, 31)
   invitations   *Would you like to come?*   (Unit 26)
                   Yes, I'd love to.
   offers   *Would you like a dessert?*   (Units 31, 34)

PRESENT SIMPLE

Positive statements

I You We They	like	York.
He She	likes	

Negative statements

I You We They	don't	like York.
He She	doesn't	

Question

Do	you we they	like jazz?
Does	she he	

Short answer Positive

Yes,	I we they	do.
	she he	does.

Short answer Negative

No,	I we they	don't.
	she he	doesn't.

1 In the 3rd person singular, *s* is added to the positive form. The 3rd person question and negative are formed with *does/doesn't* and the base form.
2 In this book, the present simple is used to express:
   personal information   *She lives in Lisbon.*   (Units 8, 30)
   likes and dislikes   *Do you like cooking?*   (Unit 9)
   fixed times   *What time do the banks open?*   (Unit 11)
   routine   *Carlos gets up at six thirty.*   (Unit 12)
   frequency   *She sometimes goes to the theatre.* (Unit 12)

PAST SIMPLE

Positive statements
I went home.

Negative statements
I didn't go home.

Question
Did you go?

Short answer: Positive
Yes, I did.

Short answer: Negative
No, I didn't.

1 The forms are the same with all subject pronouns: *I/you/he/she/it/we/they*.
2 In this book, the past simple is used to express:
   past facts   *My mother was Irish.*   (Unit 7, 19)
   past events   *We went to Florida.*   (Unit 20)
   past narrative   *I locked the door and got into bed.*   (Unit 25)
   biography   *She left school two years ago.*   (Unit 40)

PRESENT CONTINUOUS

Positive statements

I'm	writing a letter.
He's	
She's	
You're	
We're	
They're	

Negative statements

I'm	not	writing a letter.
He	isn't	
She		
You	aren't	
We		
They		

Question

Am	I	writing?
Are	you	
	we	
	they	
Is	he	
	she	
	it	

Short answer
Positive

Yes,	you	are.
	I	am.
	we	are.
	they	
	he	is.
	she	
	it	

Short answer
Negative

No,	you	aren't.
	I	'm not.
	we	aren't
	they	
	he	isn't.
	she	
	it	

In this book the present continuous is used to express:

present activities	*They're watching TV.*	(Unit 15)
temporary activities	*I'm learning to fly a light aircraft.*	(Unit 30)
future arrangements	*What are you doing next weekend?*	(Unit 26)

GOING TO FUTURE (Unit 23)

Positive statements

I'm	going to leave.
She's	
He's	
It's	
We're	
You're	
They're	

Negative statements

I	'm not	going to leave.
She	isn't	
He		
It		
We	aren't	
You		
They		

Question

Are	you	going to leave?
	we	
	they	
Is	she	
	he	

Short answer
Positive

Yes,	I	am.
	we	are
	they	
	she	is.
	he	

Short answer
Negative

No,	I	'm not.
	we	aren't.
	they	
	she	isn't.
	he	

In this book the *going to* future is used to express future plans and intention.

PRESENT PERFECT SIMPLE

Positive statements

I've	finished.
We've	
They've	
She's	
He's	

Negative statements

I	haven't	finished.
We		
They		
She	hasn't	
He		

Question

Have	you	finished?
	we	
	they	
Has	she	
	he	

Short answer Positive

Yes,	I	have.
	we	
	they	
	she	has.
	he	

Short answer Negative

No,	I	haven't.
	we	
	they	
	she	hasn't.
	he	

1 In this book the present perfect simple is used to express:
   recent events   *He's broken a cup.*   (Unit 32)
   experiences   *Have you ever been to Africa?*   (Unit 33)
                   He's been to Rio twice.
2 This tense cannot be used to talk about events which happened at a specific time in the past,
   e.g. You cannot say: ~~I have finished it yesterday~~.

Irregular verbs

Verbs with no change

cost	cost	cost
cut	cut	cut
hit	hit	hit
hurt	hurt	hurt
put	put	put
shut	shut	shut

Verbs with one change

bring	brought	brought
buy	bought	bought
catch	caught	caught
feel	felt	felt
get	got	got
have, has	had	had
hear	heard	heard
keep	kept	kept
learn	learnt	learnt
leave	left	left
lose	lost	lost
make	made	made
meet	met	met
must	had to	had to
pay	paid	paid
read /ri:d/	read /red/	read /red/
say	said	said
sell	sold	sold
send	sent	sent
sleep	slept	slept
spend	spent	spent
teach	taught	taught
tell	told	told
think	thought	thought
understand	understood	understood
win	won	won

Verbs with two changes

be (am, is, are)	was/were	been
begin	began	begun
break	broke	broken
can	could	been able
choose	chose	chosen
come	came	come
do, does	did	done
drink	drank	drunk
drive	drove	driven
eat	ate	eaten
fall	fell	fallen
fly	flew	flown
give	gave	given
go	went	gone
know	knew	known
lie	lay	lain
run	ran	run
see	saw	seen
speak	spoke	spoken
steal	stole	stolen
swim	swam	swum
take	took	taken
wake	woke	woken
wear	wore	worn
write	wrote	written

Key

Unit 3: Exercise 6
1 Japanese 2 Spanish
3 Turkish 4 Greek 5 American
6 Brazilian 7 British

Fluency 6–10: Exercise 2
The correct version is TEXT A.

Unit 14: Exercise 7
Another view of the house.

Unit 17: Exercise 6
1 India 2 China 3 USA 4 Italy
5 Austria 6 Brazil/Colombia
7 Britain 8 Germany 9 Spain
10 France 11 Greece/Turkey/
Cyprus 12 Mexico 13 Russia
14 Portugal

Unit 28: Exercise 1
John Cleese (star of *A Fish Called Wanda*) is the tallest (6ft 5in), Superman (Christopher Reeve) is 6ft 4in and Princess Diana is 5ft 10in.